THE POPES

By Zsolt Aradi

SHRINES TO OUR LADY AROUND THE WORLD

THE POPES: The History of How They are Chosen,

Elected and Crowned

THE POPES

THE HISTORY
OF HOW THEY ARE CHOSEN,
ELECTED AND CROWNED

BY

ZSOLT ARADI

FARRAR, STRAUS AND CUDAHY

NEW YORK

MANUFACTURED IN THE UNITED STATES OF AMERICA
BY AMERICAN BOOK–STRATFORD PRESS, INC., NEW YORK
PUBLISHED SIMULTANEOUSLY IN CANADA
BY AMBASSADOR BOOKS, LTD., TORONTO

To Count Giuseppe Dalla Torre di Sanguinetto

In friendship and gratitude

Contents

CONTENTS

Acknowledgments

I wish to express my deeply felt gratitude to those whose advice during the writing of this book was indispensable and to those who have taken the trouble to read the manuscript and provide me with their most valuable opinions.

First of all, I want to thank Msgr. Hugh O'Flaherty, official of the Sacred Congregation of the Holy Office, Rome; Rev. Blaise Burniston of the Franciscan Friars of the Atonement Graymoor, Garrison, N. Y., presently in Rome; P. Hermann Schmidt, S.J., Professor of Liturgy at the Pontifical Gregorian University, Rome; and my friends at the *Osservatore Romano*, Vatican City.

I have to thank also Signor Luigi Felici, manager of the firm of Felici, pontifical photographers, and Signor Francesco Giordani of the firm of Foto-Attualità, Giordani, official photographer of the *Osservatore Romano*, who were helpful in selecting the proper pictures.

BOOKS CONSULTED

Annuario Pontificio per l'anno 1955. Città del Vaticano, Tipografia Poliglotta Vaticana.

A Catholic Dictionary, edited by Donald Attwater; second edition, revised. New York, Macmillan, 1954. Mr. Attwater's work was indispensable in checking the accuracy of definitions, terms, historical and liturgical details and others.

Tu es Petrus, Encyclopédie Populaire sur la Papauté. Published under the direction of M. Abbé G. Jacquemet, Librairie Bloud et Gay, Paris, 1934.

For the history of the Church I used Ludwig Pastor's *The History of the Popes,* London, 1906–33, and Ignaz Marx's *Lehrbuch der Kirchengeschichte.*

For the description of liturgical and other ceremonies I consulted: the *Acta Apostolicae Sedis;* Adrian Fortescue, *Ceremonies of the Roman Rite,* with a preface by Cardinal Bourne, London, 1918; *Liturgie, encyclopedie populaire de connaissance liturgiques,* Bloud et Gay, Paris, 1930; the *Osservatore Romano,* February-March 1939; and my own notes and articles published during the Conclave and Coronation of Pius XII, February-March 1939.

La Città del Vaticano, by Leone Gessi. Città del Vaticano, 1937.

Enciclopedia Cattolica Italiana. Città del Vaticano, 1954.

The Catholic Church in Action, by Michael Williams. Macmillan, New York, 1935.

Catholic Encyclopedia. The Gilmary Society, New York, 1907–1913.

The Listening Post, Eighteen Years on Vatican Hill, by Thomas B. Morgan. Putnam, New York, 1944.

BOOKS CONSULTED

The 1955 National Catholic Almanac, published by St. Anthony's Guild, Paterson, N. J.

L'Ordinamento della Chiesa Cattolica, by Silvio Negro. Bompiani, Editore, Milan, 1950.

Wie die Kirche regiert wird, by Heinrich Scharp. Verlag Joseph Knecht Carolus Druckerei, Frankfurt am Main, 1950.

Die Katholische Kirche als Weltreich, by Roderich von Kienitz. Europa-Archiv, Oberursel (Germany), 1948.

The Government of the Catholic Church, by Elisabeth Linskey. Kenedy, New York, 1952.

A Papal Chamberlain, The Personal Chronicle of Francis Augustus MacNutt. Edited by Rev. J. J. Donovan; foreword by Cardinal Hayes; preface by G. K. Chesterton. Longmans, Green, New York, 1936.

Il Papato, by Paolo Brezzi. Editrice Studium, Rome, 1951.

Papstanekdoten, by Alfons Meyer. Pilger Verlag, Speyer, 1954.

La Corte Pontificia e il Cerimoniale delle Udienze, by Ferruccio de Carli. Bardi Editore, Rome, 1952.

Il Vaticano (La Corte Pontificia e Le Principali Cerimonie), by Renzo Dore. Cavalotti Editore, Milan, 1948.

Pietre, Figure, Storie e Storielle della Vecchia Roma. Vallecchi Editore, 1954.

Introduction

FOR nearly two thousand years the Papacy's role in the world has been a matter of discussion, sometimes calm, sometimes heated. The Pope is absolute spiritual ruler of four hundred seventy million Catholics * and any utterance of his is heard all over the world, in the throbbing industrial centers of Europe and North America, in the small poor villages of the Andes, in the Near and Middle East, in the remotest jungles of Africa and Brazil. Wherever his words penetrate, people take a stand. Those who belong to his flock, the Catholics, accept his statements with reverence. Others, people of good will who do not believe in the teachings of the Church of which the Pope is head, listen with the interested respect due to a person whom millions venerate. Still others, of course, are overtly or covertly hostile.

The personalities of modern popes have been well known. For example, people in this country years ago grew familiar with the figure of Pius XII, who had traveled widely

* From the *National Catholic Almanac,* 1955 (figures of 1954).

through the world, including the United States. However, the precise nature of the powers of the Pope is unknown to many and there are other questions of interest which are not well understood: How does a Pope become a Pope? Who chooses him? How secret is his election? Why is he crowned? Who crowns him? What is the significance of the ceremonies connected with his public appearances?

This book does not propose to recount the history of the Papacy or of the Catholic Church and does not propose to answer every question concerning the organization of the Church and the function of the Vatican. It does attempt to present, against the historical background, a survey of the Pope's spiritual and temporal office.

It should be well understood that it is written by a Catholic who accepts the teachings of the Church. It does not, however, deal extensively with Church doctrines and, when necessary, it seeks to explain, for non-Catholic as well as Catholic readers, what any particular doctrine—always one connected with the Papacy, the Vatican or the person of the Pope—means and why Catholics believe in it.

When the expression "Catholic Church" is used, the author always means the Roman Catholic Church, including many millions of Catholics of non-Latin rites who, though they may differ on administrative, liturgical and sometimes disciplinary matters, regard the Pope as the Supreme Head of the Church and accept the teachings of the Catholic Church which issue from Rome.

The word "Rome" always means the actual city of Rome. "Papal States" means those states which were under the temporal power of the Pope until 1870, when they became integral parts of Italy. "Vatican" means the historic Vatican Palaces and the gardens; sometimes it also means the seat of the central government of the Church. "Vatican City" means the Sovereign and Independent State of the Vatican City as established by the Lateran Treaty of 1929 between the Italian Government and the Holy See.

Strictly speaking, the word "See," which comes from the Latin word *sedes* (seat), refers to the Episcopal throne for each Bishop in his cathedral of his diocese. In present ecclesiastical usage "See" means "the charge of a Bishop, which in its territorial aspect is called the diocese." * "The Holy or Apostolic See" is the See of Rome, the Pope and his court.

This See is Holy because it is the See of the Vicar of Christ. It is Apostolic because it was the See of St. Peter, the Prince of the Apostles, the predecessor of all legitimately elected popes.

The word "prelate" could mean any high ecclesiastical dignitary, including a Bishop, but it is not used to indicate a Bishop in this book.

Other expressions and names are fully explained in the text.

* *A Catholic Dictionary,* edited by Donald Attwater. Macmillan, 1954.

THE POPES

THE POPES

CHAPTER I

The Pope and the Papacy

1. *Setting the Scene*

Rome, the center of Christian tradition, includes within its limits a small territory known as the State of the Vatican City. Insignificant in size (about forty-four hectares in area, with approximately 500 inhabitants), it is the heart of the Catholic Church, the seat and residence of its Supreme Pontiff, who is the spiritual ruler of approximately four hundred and seventy million human beings.

To Catholics, the ground of the tiny territory is sacred. It is the site of the execution of the first Christian martyrs under the Emperor Nero and the place where St. Peter, the Prince of the Apostles, whom Christ Himself designated to head His Church, was crucified. When it was certain that he would be put to death, St. Peter, the first Pope, out of humility and reverence for his Divine Master, asked to be crucified head downward. St. Peter is buried here and, since the time of his death in A.D. 67, his tomb has been one of the most profoundly venerated objects in all Christendom.

St. Peter's Basilica, in Vatican City, is the largest church building in the world. Its dome dominates the city of Rome. When the visitor arrives at St. Peter's Square, which the Basilica overlooks, he is emotionally moved by the ancient walls of the Vatican Palace—or Palaces, for there are several —the seat of the popes. Founded at divine command and existing from the time of St. Peter, the Papacy is a living force as well as an historical monument of world renown. It has no armies and its area is minute, yet it has outlasted empires, dictators, assaults of every kind, and even the human weaknesses of some of the popes.

Though the popes did not always reside in the palaces built on the Vatican Hill, the present Vatican City embodies all the traditions of the Papacy and there the central government of the Catholic Church is conducted. A few buildings outside Vatican City also belong to the Pope, house offices of the Church government, and thus enjoy extraterritorial rights on Italian soil.

Sooner or later the Roman sun gives a distinctive tan to buildings. St. Peter's Church and the Vatican Palaces have that golden warm color one associates with the city.

Coming from the neighborhood of Castel St. Angelo, the visitor first sees the façade of St. Peter's Basilica. Arriving at the Piazza, he faces the church and before it a space embraced by two semicircles of gigantic columns: the famous colonnade of Bernini. In the center of the Piazza stands an obelisque brought to Rome by Caligula from Egypt and on either side of it fountains cool the air during the hot summer days.

On the right of the colonnade, close to the church, there

is an entrance leading to the heart of the Vatican Palaces. At the left is another which leads to the Vatican Gardens and is the main entrance for vehicles entering Vatican City.

Looking to the right from the center of the Piazza one sees a conglomeration of buildings—the Vatican Palaces. Corridors connect St. Peter's Church with these buildings and they are also connected with one another. The oldest palaces date back to the fourth century and popes have been adding to them ever since. There are now twenty courtyards in the vast complex and about one thousand rooms, halls and chapels. In one stairway alone there are 127 steps, in another 294.

The tallest building, behind the right wing of the colonnade, houses the Pope's three private rooms. Two of his windows face the Square. When papal ceremonies are performed within the Basilica, the Pope and members of his court, without setting foot on the Piazza, proceed in solemn procession from this building to the church through stairways, halls and corridors.

To the rear of the Basilica, on the left, are the administrative buildings and apartment houses of Vatican City. Directly behind the church, on the slopes of the hill, is the palace of the little territory's Governor and the Vatican Gardens.

On the far right of the tiny state are garages, storage rooms, printing presses and barracks for the papal guards. Atop the hill the antennae of the Vatican radio remind one that the old is wedding to the new with surprising harmony.

2. *Scope of the Papacy*

The Pope, the supreme head of the Catholic Church, receives all the powers inherent in his office when he accepts his election by the Sacred College of Cardinals. No ceremony is needed to make his election valid. The Church, however, believes that the selection of the man invested with the highest spiritual dignity a Roman Catholic can attain should be made memorable, both for him and for the world. It therefore surrounds the event with a series of ceremonies equaled in splendor by none honoring any emperor or king. The Coronation of the new Pope—a symbolic act—is the culmination of these ceremonies.

For this great occasion, St. Peter's Basilica is filled to capacity with seventy-five or eighty thousand persons from all over the globe. Representatives of kings, of Christian and non-Christian governments, wait there in dignified silence. The long red robes of the Cardinals, the purple mantles of the Bishops, the white, black, brown, blue, and yellow ecclesiastical costumes of monks, nuns and priests are like waves of a multicolored sea.

While the whole world waits for one of the most solemn acts in Church history, while everyone's attention is focused in breathless expectation on the appearance of the Pope, who will be hailed in an outburst of joy, while everything is arranged to display the magnificent side of the Papacy, the new Pope himself is repeatedly and severely warned that all this—the splendor of the Coronation, the admiration of the multitude, the thousandfold expressions of veneration—all this, in the end, is as perishable as smoke.

Seated on the *sedia gestatoria*, his portable throne, borne by twelve *sediari* or bearers, the Pope is carried in procession from the Vatican Palace through halls and connecting corridors directly into the portico of St. Peter's Church, and then into the Basilica itself. Inside St. Peter's, while he is approaching the main altar under the dome, in the midst of splendor, the papal procession is stopped.

The Master of Ceremonies hands the Pope a brazier and a handful of flax. Silence falls. All eyes are turned to the Pope as he throws the flax upon the brazier, where it flares up in sudden flame. The blaze dies almost at once and leaves nothing in the air but smoke.

The Master of Ceremonies moves close to the Pope and, looking into his eyes, warns him: "Holy Father, thus ends the glory of the world." (*"Pater Sancte, sic transit gloria mundi."*)

The hands of the Pope are clasped in prayer and the procession moves a few steps forward. But the Master of Ceremonies orders a second halt. His face is even more serious, his gestures are even more solemn than before, and he calls out again: "Holy Father, thus ends the glory of the world." When the flame disappears and the smoke fades into the air, the procession again moves forward.

In a voice that is now almost a cry, the Master of Ceremonies for the third time halts the Pope's approach to the altar. The priest who reminds the Vicar of Christ that he will also die and become dust and ashes knows that this is the most important act of his life. The flames of the flax light up his face. The eyes of the Pope are downcast in deepest meditation. In silence those who are in the church bow, kneeling, their heads almost touching the marble floor. The flame lasts but a second and the smoke disappears like a gray-black butterfly.

Thus the new Pope enters the Basilica unforgettably reminded that the ovation he receives is rendered not to his person, which will become dust and ashes, but to God, whose Vicar he has been chosen.

Any new Pope is aware that, if power and glory go with the Papacy, with it also goes a heavy spiritual burden. To bear it properly one must be humble. The Pope is, according to his titles, Bishop of Rome, Vicar of Christ, Successor to the Prince of the Apostles, Supreme Pontiff of the Universal Church, Patriarch of the West, Primate of Italy, Metropolitan and Archbishop of the Province of Rome, and Sovereign of the State of the Vatican City. Despite all these titles, he signs all papal utterances, letters and declarations simply and humbly: *Servant of the Servants of God.* He never uses his family name after his election though, in an ageold ceremony, he will be addressed by his first and last names when he dies.

Few popes in history wished to become pontiffs and those few soon came to realize that, while they were called Vicars of Christ and Christ is God, in His human nature Christ was tortured, crucified and died the most shameful death of his epoch.

Pius XII, when informed of the outcome of the 1939 elections which made him Pontiff, cried out: "Lord, Thou art great and merciful. Have pity on me."

St. Gregory the Great, a man of profound integrity, one of the most important figures of the early Middle Ages, when elected in 590 escaped from Rome, hiding in a wicker basket used for the transport of produce. He wandered three days and three nights in forests and caves in the vicinity of Rome to avoid accepting the throne. After long meditation, however, he humbly submitted himself to the will of God.

Before the election of Pius X in 1903, the Conclave on the first ballot showed a preference for Cardinal Rampolla, though he did not have the required two-thirds majority. Rampolla prayed for hours to avert final "success." The second ballot brought the requisite majority to Cardinal Sarto who, according to eyewitnesses, had the most tortured night of his life, imploring the Almighty to save him from the burden of the Papacy.

Once elected Cardinal Sarto, as Pius X, lived the simplest of lives. In 1954, only thirty-two years after his death, he was canonized, the first Pope elevated to sainthood since 1712.

Present-day problems of Christianity and of the secular world converge toward Rome in a sharper and clearer line than anywhere else on the globe.

"Every sort of business is transacted at the Vatican," wrote a keen American observer of Church life *—"the business of State, with its multiple consequences in the temporal order; the business of intelligence, of souls, of truth and doctrine, the examination of questions of philosophy, theology and social order. From the Vatican are issued the papal utterances of various types, some of them solely concerned with subjects relating to Catholics as such, many others dealing with the most difficult problems of today and of all time.

* *The Catholic Church in Action*, by Michael Williams. Macmillan, New York, 1935.

[25]

All alike are based upon immutable principles, founded upon divine authority. From the tribunal of the Papacy thousands of decisions are made, bringing the Christian souls peace and joy, or else fear and remorse and sometimes revolt. . . . Rome has drawn all to itself, that all might be unified and vivified; it is the center from which flows and to which returns the current of spiritual life."

And of all these offices, of all this activity occurring in Rome in the Vatican, the Pope is the uncontested arbitrator.

Wherever a Pope looks from the windows of his private apartment facing St. Peter's Piazza he is confronted with evidence drawn from the pontificates of his predecessors, reminders which help him to visualize the never-ending problems he was chosen to resolve. Standing there on an early morning when sightseers stare at the building, he can recall that not so long ago, in September 1943, the border between Italy and the State of the Vatican City suddenly was occupied by Nazi SS paratroopers armed with submachine guns. In the suburbs of Rome the fight between the invaders and populace still went on. For days it was uncertain whether or not this protection, as it was called, would be converted into a new captivity, whether or not the protectors would openly invade Vatican City, as many extremist Nazis advocated.

A Pope will remember the four bombs which were dropped on Vatican territory from a Nazi airplane one night during World War II. The bombs could have brought destruction to St. Peter's, but fortunately missed it and died in the clay of the Vatican Gardens.*

---

* The engineers of the criminal idea did not want to destroy St. Peter's Church. Their aim was to make believe the Allied (British) forces bombed

THE POPE AND THE PAPACY

The little territory called Vatican City is not the creation of ambitious popes seeking worldly power but the creation of necessity. As long as the Roman Empire existed, the Pope as Bishop of Rome—though having his own means from earliest times—was protected by the Empire's might. In the chaos of the declining Empire, the Emperor ruled from distant Constantinople and the Pontiff's freedom was continually jeopardized.

After several barbaric invasions which threatened to make the Pope a satellite, Pope Stephen III decided to seek the protection of a Christian king, Pepin the Short, the father of Charlemagne, King of France.

Traveling from Rome to France in 754, Stephen III, in robes of deep mourning, his head covered with ashes, threw himself at the King's feet and implored him, in the name of the Almighty and the Apostles Peter and Paul, to intervene to save the "affairs of St. Peter and Paul and that of the community of Rome." Thus Rome and parts of the Italian peninsula, under the protection of Pepin and his successors, became the possession of the popes.

After a peace made with Emperor Constantine in the fourth century, the popes had received an endowment called the Patrimony of St. Peter's, about three hundred thousand acres around Rome. After the settlement with Pepin the Short, the Papal States consisted of this Patrimony of St. Peter's and the Romagna province of Italy. The pontiffs did not actually govern these territories until the fifteenth century.

---

the Vatican. For this purpose they used British-manufactured bombs captured in Tobruk.

At their largest, in the eighteenth century, the Papal States comprised seventeen thousand square miles and three million inhabitants. They included the duchies of Romagna, Urbino, Spoleto, Piacenza, Parma, Modena and Castro, the March of Ancona and the provinces of Bologna, Orvieto and Perugia. In 1870 all of these were annexed to the unified Kingdom of Italy and thus the Pope had no territory. His temporal sovereignty was re-established by a pact called the Lateran Treaty—because it was signed in the Lateran Palace in Rome—negotiated between Italy and the Holy See in 1929.

Several times kings and governments have offered protection to the Pope when danger arose. The offers, not always unselfish, in some cases would have involved submission to secular authority. However, Pius IX received generously disinterested offers of protection from the British Government and later from the Government of the United States. The United States had established consular offices in the Papal States as early as 1797 and in 1848 President Polk, with the consent of Congress, had created the first legation in Rome.

In 1863 when the armies of Victor Emmanuel I and Garibaldi, striving to bring the whole peninsula under one ruler, invaded the Papal States, Prime Minister Lord Russell of Britain wrote to Cardinal Antonelli, Papal Secretary of State, and offered the island of Malta as a haven for the Pontiff.

The British Premier ordered the Admiralty to be prepared to send a naval squadron to Civitavecchia, the principal port of the Papal States, to wait there for the Pope. In Malta, Lord Russell wrote to Antonelli, "His Holiness might be surrounded by his chief Cardinals and most trusty counselors. He would not be asked to subscribe to any conditions repugnant to his conscience." The offer promised complete protection of the Pope's person.

Later when the situation grew even more precarious, Rufus King, United States Minister accredited to the Papal States, took the initiative. One of the highest Vatican officials told King that probably "the only country in which the Pope could seek and find a suitable and secure asylum is the great Republic of America." King's formal offer said: "Our country is the home of civil and religious liberty as well as the refuge to all who have fled from political and other troubles in the Old World. His Holiness, should he see fit to go to the United States, would, no doubt, meet with a kind welcome and be left to pursue, unquestioned and unmolested, his great work as Head of the Catholic Church." *

King proposed that the United States send warships to Civitavecchia to await the papal decision. Secretary of State Seward approved the proposal and Assistant Secretary of the Navy Fox, at that time visiting in Rome, instructed Admiral Goldsborough, commander of the United States Mediterranean Fleet, then anchored in Lisbon, to dispatch two ships to Civitavecchia immediately. Two destroyers soon arrived at the papal port.

Pius IX, however, had no intention of abandoning Rome. Later, in 1867, when Garibaldi with a small force was only fifteen miles away from the Vatican and the sound of artillery was heard in the capital of Christianity, the Pope told

* *The Listening Post,* by Thomas B. Morgan. G. P. Putnam's Sons, New York, 1944.

some of his entourage: "Yes, I hear them coming." Then he pointed to a crucifix. "This will be my artillery," he said.

It was not until sixty years after Victor Emmanuel's troops occupied the Papal States that another Italian Government, under Victor Emmanuel III and Mussolini, signed the Lateran Treaty which, restoring the full temporal sovereignty of the popes, created the State of Vatican City. Since then the independence of this little state has been respected.

That sovereignty is essential to the performance of a Pope's spiritual mission. Some countries would send ambassadors to the Holy See even if the little state did not exist. Others—among them countries like Egypt, India, Pakistan, Japan and Great Britain—benefit from the fact that the Pope has territorial sovereignty too. These non-Christian and Protestant countries, which desire close connections with the Papacy, recognize the Pope as the head of a state instead of recognizing him as Vicar of Christ.

Papal diplomacy has a long history and is often considered the most experienced in the world. It was St. Leo the Great (440–461) who first felt the necessity of having a representative at the court of the Byzantine Emperor. He sent a so-called *apocrisarius* (the name comes from the Greek and means "the answerer") whose duty was to make reports on the situation in the court in Constantinople. Later, when a Pope sought contact with another court, he would send a *nuntius,* which in Latin means messenger. This is the origin of the name nuncio, now given to papal diplomats.

When the correspondence of Gregory the Great (590–604) with foreign courts became so large that he could not handle it alone, he created a so-called Office of Correspondence, the prototype of the present Secretariat of State of the Vatican. Pope Nicholas III (1277–1280) dispatched an envoy to Mongolia. Pope Nicholas IV (1288–1292) sent one to China. The office of permanent diplomatic representative, however, was not established until the reign of Alexander VI, the Borgia Pope (1493–1503). Ever since, papal representatives have exercised great influence in world affairs. Nothing better illustrates the Holy See's prestige than the fact that since the Congress of Vienna in 1815 the nuncios, wherever stationed, are usually the deans of the diplomatic corps.

Great popes of modern times have held office as nuncios for years before becoming Cardinals; the position has enabled them to acquire experience of the world. Leo XIII (1878–1908) was once nuncio in Brussels. Benedict XV (1914–1922) also served in the papal diplomacy. Pius XI (1922–1939) was nuncio in Warsaw during the Bolshevik invasion. Pius XII served as nuncio in Bavaria (1917–1918), and after World War I as nuncio for all Germany (1919–1929), and as papal legate (emissary) visited the United States, Latin America and other areas.

Not all papal diplomats are Italians. The Pontifical Academy includes men of many nationalities. Among them are several Americans who served in the papal foreign service in Rome or elsewhere. The first American to receive a papal diplomatic appointment was Bishop John England of Charleston, S. C., who in 1833 was sent as Apostolic Delegate to Haiti. The first American by birth who received a papal diplomatic appointment was William Cardinal O'Connell, named while he was Bishop of Portland, Maine. Pius X made him a special envoy to the Emperor of Japan. The first

American who received a so-called permanent appointment from the Holy See was Edward Cardinal Mooney, now Archbishop of Detroit. In 1930, Pius XI sent him to India as Apostolic Delegate, and in 1931 to Japan in the same capacity. The first American officially attached to the Vatican's Secretariat of State was Francis Cardinal Spellman. His seven years in Rome (1925–1932) brought about a fuller realization of the importance of Catholicism in the United States. At this writing, Archbishop Aloisius J. Muench, Bishop of Fargo, N. D., is Apostolic Nuncio for Germany, in Bonn, and Archbishop Gerald P. O'Hara, Bishop of Savannah-Atlanta, Ga., is nuncio for Eire, in Dublin.

3. *Papal Powers and Duties*

The papal audiences never end. As Vicar of Christ and head of the entire Catholic Church, the Pontiff at regular intervals receives the heads of the government of the Church, who are all located in Rome: the chiefs of the various congregations, offices and tribunals; the "Generals" of the religious orders; the presidents of the great pontifical universities run by the Jesuits, Dominicans and Benedictine Fathers; the leaders of the institutes of almost all areas, among them the North American, Latin American, Russian, German, French, Ethiopian and Philippine, as well as those institutes at which priests from Africa, China, Japan and India receive specialized training.

The Pope receives Bishops from all over the world. The Bishops are the pillars of the Catholic Church and every fifth year each will try to report to the Pontiff on the spiritual welfare of his flock. Furthermore, Bishops must report in person every five years for dioceses situated in Europe, every ten years for others. Some Bishops will not be able to appear at all; for example, those who are held by Communists or are not allowed to leave their countries.

Finally in mass, special or private audience, the Pope will try to receive every single one of the faithful who wishes to see him.

As successor of St. Peter, the Holy Father is not only Bishop of Rome but also has jurisdiction over the Universal Church. Thus he has jurisdiction over, and may have direct contact with, any Catholic without the diocesan Bishop acting as intermediary.

People will come from the remotest corners of the earth on pilgrimages to the See of St. Peter. Literally millions will come, and he will have something to say to each of them. In the opinion of the faithful, he bestows on them the greatest gift one human being can grant to another: the Apostolic Blessing imploring the grace of God.

The Apostolic Blessing or Benediction is the solemn public blessing with plenary indulgence which before 1870 the Pope pronounced from St. John Lateran on Pentecost or Ascension Day; from St. Peter's Church on St. Peter and Paul's Day, Easter Day and Maundy Thursday; and from St. Mary Major Church on the Assumption. The Pope now pronounces it whenever he wishes. The power to bestow this blessing is given by the Pope to Bishops and other prelates twice a year and to priests on special occasions.

"Blessing is a rite by which the Church dedicates persons, places or things to a sacred purpose, or attaches to them a spiritual value without consecration. . . . Consecration is an act by which a person or thing is set apart for some religious office, state or use. It is superior to and more solemn than a blessing. A priest, for example, may be consecrated, or a Bishop. Almost anything can be blessed—a house, a church, a person." *

A Pope receives almost anyone who seeks an audience regardless of the person's creed. Most of the visitors come in groups with their spiritual leaders, perhaps with a parish priest or bishop who arranges the meeting. Those who come unaccompanied go to their countries' diplomatic representatives at the Vatican who arrange the audience by applying to the office of the *Maestro di Camera* of His Holiness (chamberlain).

But anyone can present himself at the gates of the Vatican; he will be led to the office of the *Maestro di Camera* and a date will be set on which the Pontiff will receive him.

The Pope receives in *private* audience as a routine only official visitors. He also receives Cardinals, Bishops, and other ecclesiastics or laymen whose private reception for one reason or another is deemed advisable. At *special* audiences people stand in small groups and the Pope addresses each group or individual separately. At *general* audiences, which sometimes last many hours, the Pope may talk to several people separately as he walks through the crowd, but addresses the multitude and not the individuals.

In 1950, Pius XII received two circus clowns, one of them a Catholic, the other not. In Rome for the first time, they were ill at ease, wondering how the Pope would feel about

* *A Catholic Dictionary* (see Acknowledgments).

their profession. The Pontiff was informed of their uneasiness and when he met them, said: "You have a beautiful task. It is a great deed in these days to make people laugh. Real humor has the most salutary effect on the human being."

So saying, he began to impart the Apostolic Benediction but stopped when he noticed that the non-Catholic looked embarrassed. Understanding the young man's confusion, the Pope said: "The Benediction, my son, is meant for your Catholic friend. You, I hope, will accept the blessing of an old man."

Like his other powers, the spiritual power enabling the Pope to impart the Apostolic Blessing was transferred to him by his election. He is now in "the fullness of his powers." In matters of faith, morals and discipline, his authority pervades all aspects of the life of the Church. The only validly and lawfully ordained Catholic priest is one who was ordained by a Bishop who is in union with the Pope.

The human conduct of some popes has been condemned by both the world and the Church. There were some that did not live exemplary lives but, when one considers their number, these were few.

Were these popes infallible? The Catholic answer is: Yes. None of them tried to justify his conduct. They knew that they were sinners, as, without exception, we all are. This inner attitude, however, would not make them infallible. The important thing is that, in ecclesiastical matters, they did nothing and published no document which could be censored. They were mindful of the integrity of the faith.

Papal infallibility, though officially declared as recently as

1870, is not a new "law," but an essential principle of the Church. This principle (dogma) always existed and other dogmas existed also (as an appleseed holds all the energies, branches and future fruit of an apple tree). When the Church was small and restricted to Rome, it was the seed of the Church of the future ages. The first popes held all those rights the Pope has now; they did not have to be specially declared.

Infallibility applies usually to statements on matters of faith and morals, made in solemn *ex cathedra* declarations; i.e., when the Pope declares that he will make an infallible pronouncement. These *ex cathedra* declarations on faith and morals are held infallible by the whole Catholic world. But there were very few infallible papal declarations; some popes died without having ever made any *ex cathedra* pronouncement. Other papal utterances are regarded by the faithful with respect because of the Pope's function as Supreme Teacher. Any Catholic who does not accept an infallible *ex cathedra* declaration falls into heresy. It is not heresy, however, if one does not accept an ordinary routine declaration of a Pope.

In his book *The Catholic Church in Action,* Michael Williams wrote: "Perhaps most difficult for non-Catholics to understand is the acceptance of the infallibility of the Pope. It should be borne in mind that a very real distinction exists between what might be termed the functioning of the popes in their spiritual and moral capacity as the visible head of Christ's Church on earth, the extent and scope of their authority to teach and govern, and the frailties or even the gross sins of many of them as human beings. Despite the fact that the pontifical throne has been besmirched by the private lives of (some) pontiffs . . . Catholics hold that these popes did not err in matters of dogma nor did they attempt by any pronouncement to justify their own conduct."

"The bulls of these monsters," as Joseph de Maistre, French historian, tells us, "were irreproachable."

"God," said Saint Robert Bellarmine, a great Jesuit scholar, "doubtless wished to show that the power of Rome did not owe its conservation to human direction nor to prudence, and that the rock on which it rests is so strongly fortified by a singular protection of God that the powers of Hell could not prevail against it."

The Vatican Council has declared that when the Pontiff speaks *ex cathedra*, "that is, when he, using his office as shepherd and teacher of all Christians, in virtue of his Apostolic authority, defines a doctrine of faith or morals to be held by the whole Church, he, by the divine assistance promised him in blessed Peter, possessess . . . infallibility."

The burden that all popes feel often draws them to Peter's tomb under the main altar of the Basilica to seek guidance for the future from the past. When Christ founded the Church, he did not begin with an order. He asked Peter, "Do you love me?" So love of God and one's fellow beings is one message that comes from the ages, and spiritual power is essentially love.

The tombs of most of the popes are also in the Basilica. Of the first sixty popes, all but three become martyrs and saints. They suffered and died for the love of God and man. Yet in a sense they were fortunate; many popes feel that their constant and inevitable dealing with the world conceals a danger greater than martyrdom. Pope St. Pius V (1566–1572) put it clearly when he said: "As long as I lived in my cell in the monastery (he was a Dominican monk) I felt safe for my salvation. When I was appointed Bishop, my certainty started to fade, and, as Pope, I am not safe at all about my own salvation."

Walking back from the tomb of St. Peter through the solitude of the Basilica, a Pope is reminded of many tasks he is expected to fulfill. With what objectives is he to use his power? Is he to build great churches like this Basilica? Or sponsor works of art like Michelangelo's Pietà, there in a corner? In all ages, pontiffs have given artists handsome rewards and opportunities. It would be vain to try to enumerate the riches of the Vatican museums and of museums elsewhere which contain works of art stolen from the Holy See through the centuries.

The great churches and great art had one purpose: to adorn the center of Christianity, to glorify the spot toward which millions turn with reverence.

It was Pope St. Symachus (494–514) who began to rebuild the Basilica erected in the fourth century by the Emperor Constantine upon the tomb of the Prince of the Apostles. Each Pope has added something to it and all the popes have felt about it as did Pius XII, who asked the world during World War II: "How could we believe that anyone would dare to turn Rome, this noble city, which belongs to all times and all places, on which the whole civilized world fixes its eyes with trepidation, to turn her, we repeat, into a field of battle, perpetrating an act as inglorious militarily as it is abominable in the eyes of God and to humanity conscious of the highest spiritual and moral values?"

From earliest times, the Church and the popes have been repositories of cultural values. They taught Western humanity to write and to think; throughout the Middle Ages they were the founders of universities and promoters of law; they sent the first explorers to Africa, India, China, Mongolia and Japan as well as to North and South America. Their emissaries the missionaries cared for the souls and for the material well-being of men in many lands.

The humanitarian mission of the popes was most evident during the centuries when no Red Cross or other great welfare agencies existed. The Holy See was then practically the only source from which the poor and distressed could expect hope and aid. In modern times, popes have continued to extend help to the needy, sometimes even to Christianity's greatest enemies.

In the Basilica, the funerary monuments of Benedict XV and Pius XI remind us of the pontifical mission sent to Soviet Russia during the terrifying famine of the 1920's. The Moscow government finally agreed to accept foreign aid from whatever source and, together with the International Red Cross and representatives of the western powers, the Holy See dispatched a welfare mission to Russia. It was led by an American Jesuit, Father Edmund Walsh of Georgetown University. After the mission left, *Pravda,* the official Soviet newsorgan, instead of expressing gratitude, stated that the Pope (Pius XI) should be condemned to death.

Thousands of tons of food, clothing and medical supplies were distributed while the Moscow rulers continued to rain blows on Christianity and religion in general. Scholars of the Papacy remember Christ's words to Peter the Apostle: "Feed my lambs . . . feed my sheep." They help to explain why popes have taken a profound interest in social conditions and in the material welfare of the masses.

Through the ages, the form of their activity has varied according to changing human and international conditions.* From the fifteen century to the eighteenth, it took the form of rallying the western world to defend itself against the onslaught of the Turks. At other times it has taken the form of arbitration in disputes between nations. When a boundary conflict arose among Philip II of Spain, Henry IV of France and Carlo Emmanuel of Savoy, Clement VIII (1592–1604) intervened and almost miraculously achieved an agreement.

Urban VIII (1623–1644) made an effort to end the Thirty Years' War. He sent many messages and emissaries to Cardinal Richelieu, the French leader, to Gustavus Adolphus, King of Sweden, then issued a strongly worded papal bull (1632) requesting the belligerents to submit to arbitration. In 1697, Innocent XI stepped between Louis XIV of France, William of Orange and Charles II of Spain, and his mediation succeeded.

All popes recognize their mission as peacemakers. Despite the seemingly deep rifts among the Christian churches, non-Catholic religious leaders recognize it also. When Pope Pius

* During and after World War II, the Office of Information (for POW's, DP's, etc.) handled over 10 million requests from all over the world.

XII was crowned in 1939, with war clouds gathered densely on the horizon, for the first time in history the non-Catholic Orthodox Patriarch of Constantinople sent an official representative to the Coronation. And in March 1939, the Anglican Archbishop of Canterbury made the following declaration in the House of Lords: "If His Holiness would give the lead, I can promise that all the leaders of the Anglican, Orthodox and Protestant churches would give their support."

Pius XII gave the lead. Heads and members of other churches did their best to prevent the war. But no one could stop the elements let loose by satanic forces. And we may speculate but do not know the reasons why God permitted the storm.

Popes have given crystal-clear testimony about their feelings toward war and peace. When St. Pius X, a humble, soft-spoken Pope, usually full of humor, was asked by the Austrian Ambassador to bless the armies of the Hapsburg Empire at the outbreak of World War I, he was righteously indignant.

"Please, leave! Leave immediately!" he said. "I do not bless wars. I bless peace."

That was likewise the attitude of Benedict XV, who succeeded St. Pius X. Benedict ran into difficulties because in the Treaty of London, concluded in 1915, the governments of France, Great Britain and Russia agreed to "support Italy in preventing the representatives of the Holy See from taking any steps whatever in regard to the conclusion of peace or the settlement of questions connected with the present war."

[41]

Benedict, however, did not abandon his efforts to end the bloodshed. His nuncio in Berlin, at that time Archbishop Pacelli (later Pius XII), presented peace proposals from the Pontiff to the Kaiser.

Archbishop Pacelli found it difficult to pass his peace proposals to the Kaiser, who was wearing his full dress uniform. The German emperor held his sword and helmet in one hand; since the other hand had been useless since birth he could not reach for the paper. Pacelli therefore read the proposals aloud. The Kaiser said he would have them studied. But nothing happened and the war continued.

In 1918 Archbishop Pacelli was nuncio in Munich when the collapse of Germany in World War I transferred power for a brief period into the hands of Communists. Armed with guns and knives, they invaded the nuncio's home and were ready to kill him.

"Why have you come armed?" the Archbishop asked them, and added: "This is a house of peace, not a den of murderers." Much of Pacelli's life, as nuncio and as Pius XII, was spent in a heroic effort to save or restore peace.

"It is more glorious to kill war through words than to kill men through iron, and to obtain peace through peace rather than through war," said Pius XII in 1928. This practical expression of the love of God and love of neighbor is a most important part of the mission of the Papacy.

CHAPTER II

Sede Vacante
(*Vacancy of the Holy See*)

1. *The Death of a Pope*

UNINTERRUPTED succession of the Papacy is assured by rules which regulate every step from the moment of the death of one Pope until the election and Coronation of the next. These rules are the result of two thousand years of historical development and have been amplified by one Pope after another. They are now contained in the Apostolic Constitution issued by Pius XII in 1945.

The interval between the death of a Pope and election of another is called the *Sede Vacante* (Vacancy of the Holy See). During this Vacancy the deceased Pope's body is transported first to the Sistine Chapel and then to St. Peter's Church. Usually he is buried within three days after his death. Funeral ceremonies include nine days of mourning beginning on the day after the Pope dies; on each day a Cardinal celebrates a Requiem Mass for the salvation of the Pontiff's soul.

On the day after the Pope dies, moreover, preparations begin for the Conclave which will elect his successor. The following pages describe each of these steps in detail.

The Church, of which the dying Pope was not only Supreme Pontiff but also a member, takes him into her care from the moment when hope for his life is abandoned. All popes are familiar with the words of St. Augustine: "However innocent your life may have been, no Christian ought to venture to die in any other state than that of a penitent." Hence the Pope receives Extreme Unction as does any other Catholic whose last minutes approach. The only difference is that this Sacrament is administered to the Pontiff—if possible—by the Cardinal Major Penitentiary.*

Among the first to arrive at the deathbed are the Penitentiaries, the black-robed friars who are members of the Conventual branch of the Franciscans and who hear confessions in all languages in St. Peter's Basilica. They will wash the Pope's mortal remains and, after the embalming, clothe him in papal vestments. The Penitentiaries will remain at the side of the deceased Pope until his burial.

Notified of the death, the Cardinal Camerlengo (Camerlengo means chamberlain) enters the room. He will now become the most important person in the Vatican.

Until the end of the nineteenth century, accompanied by the Master of Ceremonies and by Cardinals residing in Rome, the Camerlengo approached the bed holding a small silver hammer in his right hand. Gently he lifted from the face of the Pope the linen that covered it. While all present

* *Cardinalis Poenitentiarius Major*—also translated as Cardinal Grand Penitentiary.

kneeled, the Camerlengo prayed. Then in a clear voice he pronounced the Pope's family name and baptismal name. When the cold lips failed to answer, he touched the Pope's forehead with the silver hammer. Three times, in the profoundly silent room, he called the Pope's name and the little hammer tapped the cold forehead. Then he turned to those present and solemnly declared: "The Pope is truly dead." Notaries, the Master of Ceremonies and physicians signed the certificate of death. The Camerlengo signed it too and put his seal upon it.

Since the end of the nineteenth century the use of the silver hammer has been abandoned. The rest of the ceremony to certify the death is the same.

The Camerlengo first takes the fisherman's ring from a prelate of the Apostolic Chamber, its guardian, and removes its seal bearing the name of the dead Pope and image of St. Peter with the fisherman's net. With this ring the Pope had authenticated papal documents called Apostolic briefs (breve). Then the Camerlengo takes possession of another papal seal with which the Pope had authenticated more formal edicts, the so-called bulls. The second seal bears the Pope's name, a cross and the images of St. Peter and Paul, and is usually pressed into red ink or wax or lead. The seals must be made unserviceable so that they cannot be abused after the Pope's death.

The First General Assembly of the Cardinals is held a day after the death and before then the seals will be destroyed. The pieces will be shown to each Cardinal at the Assembly by one of the officials of the Apostolic Camera.

With the seals in his possession, the Camerlengo leaves the

papal apartment and walks through ten immense halls separating it from the rest of the Vatican. In normal times these are used as antechambers and are full of people: red-robed lay chamberlains in their Renaissance uniforms, priests of Rome, visitors waiting to see Vatican officials. Now the Camerlengo walks through the halls alone and only in the tenth does he encounter people: Swiss Guards who in this outer hall, stand watch over the papal apartment. Here two officers of the guard attach themselves to the Camerlengo and, in acknowledgment of his new dignity, accompany him during the entire time that the papal throne is vacant.

As the Camerlengo arrives at his office, the Cardinal Vicar asks that all the bells of all the churches of Rome announce the death of the Pope. When Rome was a papal dominion the Camerlengo would order that the large bell on the Capitoline Hill be sounded first and that the other bells follow the majestic, sad tones of the big bell on Rome's ancient City Hall. Now the City of Rome itself gives the order.

As long as the Papal States existed, the death of the Pontiff meant general amnesty for all minor criminals within their borders. A town crier with a drum would arrive before each prison and announce what categories of prisoners should be immediately released.

All wishes expressed in the will of the deceased Pope must be observed (there have been popes who did not wish to be embalmed). When the embalming is over, the Pontiff's body is immediately taken into the Sistine Chapel. It is vested in white with closely fitting headgear. White candles are lit at the bier. An honor guard of officers of the Noble Guard stands stiffly at attention, wearing dress uniform with a black band on the left arm.

Here the Pope lies until the next day beneath Michelangelo's gigantic frescoes representing the Last Judgment.

2. *The Papal Funeral*

On the day following the death, the whole chapter and clergy of St. Peter's Basilica, about fifty-five priests, appear at the Sistine Chapel to ask the Penitentiaries, who until now have watched the Pope's body, to deliver it to them. They do deliver it but remain close. There is no rule or order that prescribes that the Pope's body has to be buried three days after his death. Usually, however, in the evening of the day following the death, the deceased Pope's body is carried in solemn funeral procession from the Sistine Chapel to St. Peter's Basilica and exposed at the Chapel of the Most Holy Sacrament.

While the Pope's body lies in the Sistine Chapel, he is vested in his white cassock with Mozzetta and the close-fitting red velvet cap called *camauro*. Before being taken into St. Peter's Basilica, he is vested in his pontifical robes with the mitre on his head. He is buried in the pontifical robes.

In the Chapel of the Most Holy Sacrament, twenty candles are lit in candelabras, six before the bier, six on the steps on the altar, and eight, four on each side, at the catafalque.

While the body is in this chapel, the people of Rome are allowed to pass before it. Twenty-four hours or longer endless thousands take advantage of this opportunity to bid farewell to their Bishop.

The funeral Masses are said in St. Peter's, the first by the Dean of the Sacred College of Cardinals. On subsequent days Masses are said by the Cardinal Bishops and Cardinal Deacons during the last three days by three Cardinal Priests.

The ceremony of these nine-day Requiems, called novemdial, is also prescribed. The Cardinals are vested in purple mozzettas (hooded capes reaching the elbow, closed in front with buttons), *rochettos* (narrow-sleeved, knee-length garments, made of linen, the lower part lace) and birettas (three-ridged hats). All their clothes are purple—not red, the color usually associated with the dress of Cardinals—because purple is a liturgical color of mourning.

Prelates of the papal court wear black stockings and purple *cappa* (a cloak covering the whole person, worn over the other vestments). This is the dress prescribed for them during the Vacancy of the Holy See.

On the third day after the death, the Cardinals created by the late Pope carry the catafalque from the Chapel of the Most Holy Sacrament to the apse of the Basilica.

These last rites for the Pope are of somber majesty. St. Peter's Basilica is filled with people in black. During the entire ceremony of the burial an official of St. Peter's Basilica —a prelate—standing a few steps from the bier, reads in recitative the phrases of the burial ceremony. When the Archpriest starts the antiphons the reader announces it to the people. When the Pope's body is blessed, he announces it and reads the names of the Cardinals and prelates who officiate during the funeral. His voice falls when he informs the congregation that the Pope's body is being put into the first coffin. Then he stops and there is absolute silence in the

Basilica. Before the first coffin is put in the second, the loud voice starts again. "And now, the mortal remains of His Holiness."

Otherwise, the burial does not differ in form from the burial ceremony for any other Catholic.

The Archpriest's voice starts the antiphon: *"Non inters . . ."* "Enter not into judgment with Thy servant, O Lord. . . . Deliver me, O Lord, from everlasting death."

In a funeral service absolution is given to emphasize that the Church, which has the right to "bind or absolve," absolves the deceased. At the funeral service for a Pope, absolution is given by one of the Cardinals who is an Archbishop. During the *novemdiali* nine more absolutions will be given. (Five absolutions are given to a Bishop after his death.) Then three of the Cardinals who were created by the late Pope put his body into the cypress wood coffin. Into this coffin also are thrown gold, silver and copper medals bearing the image of the Pope and corresponding in number to the number of years he ruled as Pontiff.

The first Cardinal created by the Pope covers the Pontiff's face with a purple veil and the entire body with a red ermine blanket. The cypress coffin is thereupon locked and put in the lead coffin, on which is placed the Pope's coat of arms and a copy of the certificate of death. The lead coffin is sealed and the two coffins holding the body of the Pope are placed in a coffin of elmwood. (The three coffins have no liturgical meaning. Their only purpose is to conserve and protect. The reason for putting medals and coins into the Pope's coffin is to make identification in the future easier. It has happened often that the inscription on a coffin has disappeared, vestments and body perished, but coins identified the remains.)

The Archpriest's voice rises and the Basilica resounds with the words and music of the Gregorian chant: *"Circumdederunt me gemitus mortis et doloris inferni. . . ."* ("The sighs of death and the pains of Hell circle around me, O Lord. . . .")

"May the angels lead thee into Paradise," the choir sings while the body is lowered into the vault under the main altar of the Basilica. The Lord's Prayer is said and the vault and the coffins are blessed. Masons then wall up the vault and on it fasten a marble cover bearing the Pope's name.

3. *Tribute of the Diplomats*

One of the most impressive occasions following the death of a Pope is that on which tribute is paid to him and to his office by members of the diplomatic corps accredited to the Holy See.

Driving to the Vatican, the chiefs of missions and their aides enter at the St. Marta Gate, on the left of St. Peter's Basilica. Two Swiss Guards present arms and papal gendarmes halt the cars for identification. The cars stop on Martyr's Square, where the first Christian martyrs were executed.

Now the road bends and the visitors have a view of the tiny Vatican State's territory, complete with broadcasting center and railway station. Diplomats are invariably impressed as they arrive at the final archway where the intricate Vatican Palace begins. The Italian expression *sacri palazzi* (sacred palaces) is the right one, they realize.

The diplomats are received in the Sala Regia, the Royal Hall, where popes used to receive Catholic princes who expressed special devotion to the Pontiff. There is no furniture in this room. Its walls are of marble, with red brocade tapestry bearing the coat of arms of popes. Swiss Guards stand at attention as Monsignori, Masters of Ceremonies in black cassocks and Vatican ushers lead the diplomats into the room.

Large empires and small are represented, states with old tradtions and countries newly created. The diplomats stand in line, their positions determined by the length of time they have served at the Holy See. At this writing, the French Ambassador, Count Vladimir d'Ormesson, is dean of the corps.

At this writing, also, the Polish Ambassador is still the same man who was appointed in 1936. The Holy See has never recognized the Polish Communist Government and, at the Vatican, Ambassador Papèe is entitled to all diplomatic privileges. So too is the Minister of Lithuania. Like the United States, the Vatican has never accepted Soviet Russia's occupation of the Baltic States. (See Appendix IX.)

Eire has an Ambassador. Almost all the Central and South American countries have ambassadors or ministers there. Mexico, however, has none. Naturally the Philippines, an entirely Catholic country, is represented.

For many years the Netherlands did not send a diplomatic mission to the Vatican though it did accept a nuncio. Now there is a Dutch minister among the diplomats. The chief of the Swiss Guard is not a diplomat but actually represents

[51]

Switzerland and there is a nuncio accredited at the Swiss Federal Council in Berne.

Finland is almost entirely Protestant. Nevertheless it has diplomatic relations with the Holy See recognizing the Vatican's importance and it is represented by a minister. Nationalist China established diplomatic relations with the Holy See during the 1930's; after China, Japan sent a minister too.

With Lebanon, the Arab countries began to establish relations with the Pope. Egypt sent a minister next. Then the greatest Moselm state in the world, Pakistan, expressed a desire for diplomatic relations and now has a minister at the Vatican.

Next came Indonesia, then Iran and Syria, then India. Liberia and Haiti are also represented.

When all these diplomats are assembled in the Sala Regia, the Sacred College of Cardinals arrives as a body, headed by the Camerlengo, who is flanked by two Swiss Guards wearing helmets and holding halberds in their right hands.

Beside the Cardinal Camerlengo stands the Secretary of the Sacred College. During the Vacancy, he is the only one who, in case of necessity, may get in touch with the diplomats, since the Secretary of State's term of office expires with the death of the Pope and no Cardinal has the right to receive any diplomat officially.

Now stepping forward to this solemn, sorrowing audience, the dean of the diplomatic corps expresses the condolences of his colleagues.

4. *The People Sorrow*

Rome is full of legends. In many of them, pagan mythology, superstition and genuine Christian liturgy have mingled and it takes time and energy to determine what is pure imagination and what is historical fact. The Mediterranean world abounds with the shadows of Greek and Roman gods, with tales of the Phoenicians' and later the Saracens' dark violence, with memories of the medieval mind's constant struggle with the devil. Many Roman legends deal with the deaths of popes. One goes back to the tenth and eleventh centuries, to Sylvester II, the first Pope of French origin, who ruled from 999 to 1003.

Sylvester II introduced Arabic numerals into the western world, his artists constructed steam-pressured organs, and he built the first Lateran Palace (for centuries the habitation of the popes). He also built an observatory which, though primitive, made him some sort of magician in the minds of the ignorant. Many people were convinced that this Pope was elected with the help of the devil, with whom, they said, he had made a pact. One clause, however, stipulated that the pact would remain invalid if the Pope did not visit Jerusalem, and so Sylvester felt safe since he had no intention of traveling to the Holy Land.

Alas! Sylvester—and this is pure legend—had forgotten that there is a church in Rome which bears the name of Jerusalem (Santa Croce in Gerusalemme). In his forgetfulness, he celebrated Mass there and thus tumbled into the devil's trap. Immediately he felt his guilt, confessed it to the people in the church and asked them not to honor his "damned body." Then he fell dead. At this moment mysterious horses appeared which seemed to burn with flames and dragged his body to the Lateran Basilica.

Sylvester II's funeral monument was erected in the Lateran Basilica by Sergius IV. For centuries it was believed that the tombstone sweat blood. That legend died out but another remains. It holds that whenever a Pope lies dying the bones of Sylvester II begin to move and hammer the tomb with such violence that the noise is audible even outside the church.

There are other nonlegendary incidents connected with the funerals of popes and some are as dramatic as the legends themselves.

When Pius IX died in 1878, Rome was part of the Italian kingdom and the popes did not possess secular power. The adherents of the King and the followers of the defeated Papal States were not yet reconciled. Pius IX requested in his will that he be buried in the Basilica of San Lorenzo, which is about two miles from the Vatican. He was first laid to rest in one of the niches of St. Peter's Basilica and the tense atmosphere existing between the Holy See and Italy did not permit the transfer of the body before 1881.

At that time it was decided to move the Pope's remains to San Lorenzo with due escort and funeral dignity. As the funeral procession arrived at the bridge over the Tiber facing Castel St. Angelo, it was attacked by a small group of anti-Catholic desperadoes planning to seize the coffin and throw it into the river. The ensuing battle, in which eight people were killed, required the intervention of Italian police and soldiers. The coffin was rescued but it had to be rushed to the Church of San Lorenzo without further ceremony.

The last request of Pope Leo XIII (1878–1903) was that he be buried in the Lateran Basilica, but his body was not transferred there until 1925. With the consent of the Italian Government, which had not yet settled its differences with the Holy See, the transfer took place at night and without ceremony, witnessed by two Cardinals, Cardinal Gasparri and Cardinal Merry del Val. The workmen of St. Peter's Basilica, using torchlight, carried the coffin in an automobile to the Lateran Basilica where the funeral monument awaited it.

In 1922 the government of Ivanhoe Bonomi (who, incidentally, became the first Prime Minister of democratic Italy in 1943 after the Allies liberated parts of the peninsula) had shown great respect at the death of Benedict XV. Bonomi ordered that all flags on public buildings be lowered to half-mast.

In 1954, after the canonization rites of Pius X, the people of Rome performed an act of reparation for the fact that the great Pope's body could not be exposed at the St. Mary Major Basilica right after his death in 1914. The day after his canonization Pius X's body, which was buried in St. Peter's Basilica, was carried in one of the most solemn processions Rome has ever seen to the Basilica of St. Mary Major and exposed for ten days to the veneration of the people. After this, a procession not less splendid carried it back to St. Peter's.

At the death of a Pope, the people of Rome usually pay

him reverent homage. They are conscious of what the popes mean to them, and any sign that a Pope might leave the city would be received with near-terror. For the Romans the Pope is there even during the Vacancy. Their respect for the life of the Pontiff is expressed in their proverb: "The Pope is not sick until dead."

5. *Preparations for the Conclave*

During the vacancy of the Apostolic See (*Sedis vacantia*) the Cardinals become trustees of the papal authority though they cannot exercise it. The government of the Church in Rome includes twelve Sacred Congregations, three tribunals or courts, three offices and secretariats, on all of which there are Cardinals, prelates and other Church dignitaries. After the death of a Pope the Cardinal Camerlengo takes over the administration of the Holy See while the obligation of choosing the Pontiff's successor falls on the Sacred College of Cardinals. Meanwhile, life in the Vatican and in the Church administration comes almost to a standstill.

The Sacred Congregations—the departments of the Church's spiritual and material administration—restrict their activity to routine work until the election of a new Pope. The Cardinals are advisors of the Pope but he need not accept their advice. His own authority, according to Catholic doctrine, comes directly from Christ and only he can make final decisions. Thus, during the Vacancy, papal power does not reside in the College of Cardinals but is suspended. The authority is within Christ and reappears in the person of the individual who is to be elected.

No briefs, bulls or other documents are or can be issued. No new agreements with foreign states are signed, nothing is altered at the Vatican Palaces or at St. Peter's Church and no new appointments are made, even of minor lay officials. The usual bustle of activity in Vatican City ceases and the atmosphere is that of any house in which death has taken the head of the family.

That part of the Sacred College of Cardinals which resides in Rome is called the Curia. The Cardinals of the Curia are either heads, prefects or secretaries of one of the Sacred Congregation (four Sacred Congregations are headed by the Pope). The Sacred Congregations deal with problems arising within special areas of ecclesiastical jurisdiction—for example, with sacraments, ceremonies, institutions of higher learning and propagation of the faith. The tribunals concern themselves with appeals from judgments, as for example in marriage cases. The Papal Offices once had important functions. The Chancery (Cancellaria) kept the papal archives, the Datary (Dataria) took charge of expediting papal documents and decisions and put the Date (Datum) upon them, and the Apostolic Chamber (Camera) administered material affairs of the Papal State.

Originally, until the Middle Ages, it was the actual chamber in which were stored the vestments, sacred vessels and gems of the Pope. Now it is the head of this Apostolic Chamber, the Cardinal Camerlengo, who becomes the head of the administration of the Holy See. The members of the Apostolic Chamber, who during the Pope's life had other functions in the congregations and offices, become the organizers of the papal funeral and the papal election.

In the Sacred Congregations, tribunals and offices only the Cardinal Major Penitentiary can make major decisions. There are sins from which a Catholic cannot be absolved by an ordinary priest or even by a Bishop and such cases are referred to him. Because the salvation of souls cannot wait, he is authorized to decide these cases even during the Vacancy.

Daily three Cardinals assist the Camerlengo—each day another group of three. With their help and that of the members of the Apostolic Chamber, he assumes responsibility for the properties of the Holy See, the Vatican Palace, Catholic churches in and outside Vatican City, and other papal properties in Italy and in foreign countries. He will transfer them intact to the new Pope.

During the Vacancy the Cardinals hold a daily General Assembly to prepare the Conclave and deal with unavoidable problems. But the Cardinals cannot overrule anything done by the late Pope. As Pius XI phrased it: "Only the Pope may undo what the Pope may do."

It is assumed that the Cardinals will hold about ten General Assemblies. Each day they deal with a different subject. For more than two hundred years the schedule of these meetings was the following: *

First day: verification of the destroyed papal seals. Appointment of a prelate to deliver the Latin language funeral sermon after the ninth Requiem Mass which will be held for the dead Pope. Appointment of another prelate to deliver the Latin sermon after the Mass of the Holy Ghost, said just before the Cardinals enter the Conclave.

Second day: selection of the Conclave's site.

* This schedule is no longer in effect.

Third day: election of a Father Confessor to the Conclave.

Fourth day: appointment of physicians to the Conclave, as well as pharmacists and their aides.

Fifth day: appointment of barbers and waiting and service personnel.

Sixth day: distribution, by lot, of the rooms the Cardinals will occupy at the Conclave.

Seventh day: appointment of cleaning personnel and third Conclavists, in case any Cardinal requests a third aide.

Eighth day: discussion of food supply.

Ninth day: assignment of the inside keys of the Conclave, by majority vote, to the Camerlengo's aides.

Tenth day: Appointment of masons and carpenters, two of each, to be taken into the Conclave. Now all these questions are resolved in a simpler way because of the technological facilities of the modern age.

The Cardinals are bound by Church law to begin the election of a new Pope at the latest on the eighteenth day after the late Pontiff's death.

When the Cardinal Camerlengo takes over the administration of the Holy See the few documents he has to sign are sealed with a curious "coat of arms." He and other officials who play important parts during the Vacancy coin commemorative medals. On the Camerlengo's appears a big umbrella, known as *ombrellone,* the sign of the Vacancy of the Holy See.

The symbol is very old. Its exact origin is not entirely clear but it is certain that it comes from the Orient, probably from Mongolia, where it was a sign of dignity and of power, both human and divine. In Mongolia only the highest military leaders were allowed to put up tents during campaigns. The big tents of the supreme commanders were shaped like *ombrellone*.

Leaders of the Roman Empire adopted the symbol and at one time it was used to represent papal authority in general. In the Middle Ages the popes sometimes used it to symbolize the importance of the great Basilicas. Now all the Basilicas in and outside of Rome may use the sign of a smaller umbrella and the *ombrellone* remains the sign of papal authority during the Vacancy. It signifies that the papal jurisdiction is at a standstill but that the Papacy as an institution nevertheless exists. Crossed with the *ombrellone* on the Camerlengo's medal are two keys symbolizing the authority of the Pope.

Another medal issued at this time belongs to the Governor of the Conclave. This bears his name, his coat of arms, the inscription CONCLAVIS GUBERNATOR and the date, with a key to symbolize his part in locking the Conclave doors.

The Vatican State issues money in the form of coins. On one side, they bear the inscription STATO DELLA CITTÀ DEL VATICANO (State of the Vatican City) and on the other side the image of the Holy Ghost in the form of a dove. The Vatican postoffice issues new stamps bearing the inscription SEDE VACANTE.

Until a new Pope is elected, the Vatican's semiofficial daily newspaper, the *Osservatore Romano,* carries the Vacancy sign on its front page and until the burial of the Pope is bordered in black. The newspaper describes the arrivals of the Cardinals and publishes their biographies, gives detailed accounts of the current ceremonies, prints telegrams and letters sent by foreign governments. In twenty or more languages the Vatican radio carries to the remotest corners of the world news accounts of the events in Rome.

The Vatican's press office, which during normal times is at the Porta Angelica close to the *Osservatore Romano*, is transferred to larger quarters. All major international news agencies work with enlarged staffs. Broadcasting stations install wires for microphones in the Basilica, as the Camerlengo's office directs.

Everything is done in the greatest order, for the procedures have been prescribed in the Apostolic Constitution issued in December 1945. The prevailing motto is "prudence, charity and the greatest calm."

The Cardinals begin preparations for the papal election from the moment they reach Rome. Upon his arrival, each Cardinal takes his first oath, administered by the Camerlengo. He solemnly swears that he understands the laws which govern the choice of the Pope; that he will meticulously observe all rules pertinent to the election procedure; that he will also observe the secrecy of the election and, in case he himself is elected, will not surrender any temporal rights of the Holy See which are essential to the independence; that he will not become a pawn of any secular power while giving his votes to the man he chooses to become Pontiff and Vicar of Christ.

6. *History of the Conclave*

Circumstances surrounding the election of the Pope were not always as calm and orderly as they are today nor was the election always held in Rome.

The present system of election originated more than eight hundred years ago. To understand it, one must return to the earliest days of Christianity.

The first Pope, St. Peter, was not elected by the Apostles; he received his mission from the Divine Master. How his immediate successors were elected we do not know. A letter of St. Clement written in A.D. 98 to the Corinthians indicates that Bishops were elected by the clergy and the faithful. Presumably the Bishop of Rome, the head of the Church, was elected in the same way.

A century and a half later, in A.D. 251, St. Cyprian of Carthage wrote in a letter of the choice of Pope St. Cornelius who, he said, was elected—that is, made Bishop—by the "judgment of God and Christ, witnessed by almost the whole clergy (of Rome) and with the suffrage of the people present."

Thus, in ancient times, the Pope was elected like the Bishops, by the clergy and the people of Rome.

Since the entire people participated in the election, partisan factions were easily created and utilized by the ever-growing secular power. After a time, the ruler who held Rome had great and sometimes decisive influence on the election: first the western Emperors, then the Germanic (Gothic) Kings, then the Emperors of the declining Roman Empire, then the Roman nobility, the medieval Kings and later the Emperors of the Holy Roman Empire.

In the fourth century there were serious troubles. In 366 when St. Damasus, an austere Spanish monk, was elected, the party of an ambitious and vain Deacon Ursicinus, enraged by his defeat, invaded the churches and massacred the faithful by the hundreds. To avoid such occurrences the popes asked the protection of the ruler of the City, whoever he might be, but they did not abandon the principle that the right to elect the Bishop of Rome belonged, not to the ruler, but to the people and to the clergy. In brief: Until the eighth century the election of a Pope did not differ from the election of a bishop. After the eighth century, it was the clergy (Roman) who elected the Pope with the assistance of the people.

For the Papacy, the tenth century was a period of deepest humiliation. During the reign of the Corsican Pope Formosus (891–896) one of the most important offices of the papal court was confided to a certain Theophylact whose ambitious and immoral wife, Theodora, soon obtained sufficient power to meddle directly in Roman affairs. Her two daughters, Theodora the Younger and Marozia, were more ambitious still and with their mother played so prominent a part in Roman politics that in 903, on the death of Pope Leo V, the Theophylact family was in a position to control the papal elections. A month after his lawful election, Pope Leo V was dethroned, jailed, tortured and finally killed by thugs in the pay of this family. The iron century of the Papacy followed, with control in the hands of the women, Theodora and Marozia.

History, however, remembers and respects Leo I, St. Gregory the Great and other popes who ruled the Church in the same age. They imparted to the Holy See a luster which insured its prestige for generations to come.

Pope Nicholas II (1059–1061) finally put an end to the old system under which, since 769, the clergy elected the Roman Bishop. He decreed that the clergy, including the Cardinal Deacons and Cardinal Priests, could assist but that only the Cardinal Bishops could elect the Pope. Yet the decree was not always enforced. After the death of Alexander II in 1073, when the funeral of the Pope was over, the people and clergy present shouted: "Hildebrand is the Bishop." Hildebrand, a monk, one of the greatest religious figures of the Middle Ages, who worked for decades to cleanse the Papacy of undue secular influences, did not wish to accept the office. Finally Cardinals, clergy and people cried with unanimity: "St. Peter has chosen Hildebrand for Pope." Under the name of Gregory VII, the humble Hildebrand became one of the outstanding papal reformers.

Later Alexander III, in 1179, decreed that the Bishop of Rome should be elected by all three categories of Cardinals: Cardinal Bishops, Cardinal Priests and Cardinal Deacons. He also decreed that the election must be by two-thirds majority. The latter decree remained in force until December 8, 1945, when Pope Pius XII ordered that elections be by two-thirds plus at least one.

In the early part of the thirteenth century, after the death of the energetic Gregory IX (1216–1241), who successfully fought Barbarossa, canonized St. Francis of Assisi and helped to spread the Franciscan order, Barbarossa's son Manfred continued his father's attacks on the Papacy. In this extremely difficult situation the Cardinals could not find a man of sufficient strength to be the Head of the Church. Pope Celestin, elected in 1241, died almost immediately. After his death there was a Vacancy of a year and a half which ended only when the Roman Senate and the people locked the Cardinals in a fortresslike building, "the Septizonium," constructed by the Emperor Septimus Severus.

The Pope finally elected was Innocent IV, who was driven out of Rome by Manfred, son of the German Emperor Frederic II, but returned. His successor Alexander IV, also forced out of Rome by Manfred, was elected in Naples. There a determined mayor closed the gates of the city and forced the Cardinals to elect a new Pope within five days.

Alexander, who later went back to Rome, was driven out again and died in Viterbo, a city to the north. His successor, Urban IV, was elected after three months of deliberation by the Cardinals and Urban's successor Clement IV after four months. Clement died in Viterbo in 1268.

These were the most troubled times of the Middle Ages, the days of the last Crusades to secure the Holy Places in Palestine, days of upheavals in Europe and upheavals also in the souls of individuals. When Clement IV died in his palace among Viterbo's hills, the eighteen Cardinals retired to elect a new Pope but, in view of the chaotic situation in the Christian world, none of them wished to assume the terrible responsibility.

Days, then weeks, then months, then years passed, and still there was no Pope. The Christian world grew anxious and the King of France and other sovereigns visited Viterbo to urge the Cardinals to put an end to the long Vacancy. Finally St. Bonaventure advised the people of Viterbo to resort to the kind of measures the Romans and Neapolitans had practiced when the election lasted too long. The people accordingly locked the Cardinals into a palace. Even this step, however, did not hasten matters.

At this point the mayor of Viterbo, Alberto Montebono, and the captain of the municipal militia, Gallo, decided to use more energetic methods. All the entrances of the palace were walled in by masons. Food was delivered through a small rotating door. The mayor appointed a special corps under the leadership of a Marquis Savelli to guard the building so that no one could escape from it. Several Cardinals in the palace became ill and some died, but still there was no election. The mayor then ordered that the palace's roof be torn down, leaving the Cardinals exposed to the fall rains. At the same time he ordered that only bread and water be given to the electors.

The Cardinals now offered the Papacy to St. Philip Benizi, one of the greatest figures of that troubled age. Hearing of their intentions, he fled in secret and remained in solitude until another choice was made. The choice was Theobald Visconti, who was neither a Cardinal nor a consecrated priest but a papal legate in Syria. He accepted the election and later mounted the throne as Gregory X. Thus the vacancy ended after three and a half years.

Conscious of all the ills of a long Vacancy, Gregory X, in his Apostolic Constitution (*Ubi periculum*) issued in 1274, originated the Conclave (which means both the system and the place of the election). Conclave comes from the Latin word *clavis* (key) and means a locked place.

Several popes elaborated this system. Pius X adapted it to modern times and both Pius XI and Pius XII made changes in it. Fundamentally, however, the traditional ceremonies are the same as they were in 1274. Consider, for example, the function and the person of the Conclave's marshal. As has been said, the Mayor of Viterbo appointed a Marquis Savelli to be responsible for the locks and generally for the secrecy of the Conclave. The office of guardian, or marshal, remained in the Savelli family until the male branch became extinct. Then it was inherited by the Chigi family which held it until the death of Prince Chigi-Albani in 1950. When the Cardinals retire behind locked doors it is the marshal of the Conclave who, dressed in medieval robes, keeps the keys and his own flag flies upon the Vatican.

Thus a three-year-long Vacancy and the measures of the people of Viterbo finally created the Conclave form of electing popes. As a matter of fact, when Gregory X issued his Apostolic Constitution, it had already been decided that the Bishop of Rome must be elected by all the Cardinals in a place locked from the outside.

The procedures instituted by Gregory were severe. All the Cardinals were locked in one room, in which they slept, ate and conferred. Food was passed to them through a window. After the third day they received only one dish at each meal, after the eighth day only bread and water and a little wine. Later these regulations were eased but, after centuries, the basic principle of the Cardinals' absolute seclusion from the outer world remains in effect today.

Certain conclaves might well be called "dangerous" for the participants. At the election of Urban VIII in July 1623, Rome suffered from an excessive heat wave. The Conclave lasted only eleven days but many Cardinals contracted malaria and eight Cardinals and forty of their aides, the so-called Conclavists, died. Even the new Pope, only fifty-five years old, strong and healthy, caught the disease and narrowly escaped death.

The Conclave system has not always saved time. The Conclave of 1740 lasted six months. The Cardinals were tired, many ill, but there was no solution in sight. Then—as told—one Cardinal Lambertini, known for his humor and at the same time for his pious life, jokingly said to the assembly: "We ought to make an end now. . . . If you want a saint, elect Cardinal Gotti; if you want a statesman, elect Cardinal Aldrovandi; but if you are ready to be satisfied with an honest fellow, here I am." And history teaches us that Lambertini was chosen and that the choice was a wise one.

One of the great trials of the modern Papacy occurred in the French Revolutionary and Napoleonic era, after 1789. Bonaparte's army invaded the Papal States, then under Pius VI (1775–1799), and in the treaty of Tolentino demanded probably the greatest ransom in history, including the transfer to the French of all works of art in the Vatican Palace (most of them are now in the Louvre). When his chief delegate in Rome was assassinated, Napoleon arrested the Pope. Pius VI died heartbroken as a poor exile in France. Before his death, however, he managed to write a letter to his trusted Minister Consalvi (who later became Cardinal Secretary of State), telling him what to do in case of a Vacancy.

Consalvi was in jail but succeeded in escaping and reached Venice in disguise. From there he sent out a call for the Sacred College and the Conclave was held in Venice in March 1800. The new Pope, Pius VII, was crowned in Venice in St. Mark's Basilica. But now the Austrian government protested, declaring that the Coronation is a symbol of temporal power but that, with the Pope driven out of Rome and his state in the hands of the French, he did not possess territorial sovereignty.

About a hundred years later the Austrian Government again tried to interfere with a papal election. When the Conclave which followed the death of Leo XIII began on July 30, 1903, it seemed almost certain that Leo's Secretary of State, Cardinal Rampolla, would be chosen to succeed him. Suddenly Cardinal Puszyna, Archbishop of Cracow (now in Poland but at that time part of Austria), arose and, addressing his "Venerable Brethren, Lord Cardinals of the Holy Roman Church," said he had been instructed by his august Sovereign, His Imperial Majesty, Francis Joseph, the Emperor of Austria and King of Hungary, that if Cardinal Rampolla received the number of votes necessary to elect him, the King-Emperor would "exercise his power of veto."

This Right of Exclusion, commonly called veto, actually existed and was occasionally exercised by the Catholic powers but the custom had been discontinued long since.

Cardinal Rampolla protested against Austria's interference, not out of self-interest but to preserve the Conclave's rights. The Polish Cardinal of Cracow, however, was firm. The Conclave could not and did not elect Rampolla. In his stead it elected Giuseppe Sarto, the Patriarch of Venice.

Leaving Venice on his way to the Conclave in Rome he had bought a round-trip ticket at the railway station. Now he was the Pope (known since 1954 as St. Pius X). One of his first acts was to abolish the all-but-forgotten veto right. And as a contemporary witness wrote after the Conclave which elected Pius X, "Bishop Merry del Val talked to Puszyna as probably no Cardinal had ever before been spoken to in the Vatican. Even the Borgia rooms had never echoed to such language."

CHAPTER III

A Pope Is Elected

1. The Procession to the Conclave

Now the great day has arrived, the last of the novemdiali has been celebrated and the Cardinals are ready to enter the Conclave.

As has been said, all the Cardinals—seventy—enjoy the right to take part in the election. Even a Cardinal who had been excommunicated, suspended or indicted must vote and could be voted for.

Until 1922 the prescribed interval between the death of a Pope and the beginning of the Conclave was ten days. On the eleventh day the voting began. In 1914 Cardinal Gibbons of Baltimore, Cardinal O'Connell of Boston, and Cardinal Begin of Quebec did not arrive in time for the election of Benedict XV. In 1922 Cardinal O'Connell arrived after the first Cardinal Deacon had announced that Cardinal Ratti, Archbishop of Milan, had become Pontiff under the name of Pius XI. Under Pius XI the interval was changed to fifteen days—eighteen, if necessary.

[71]

On the day they enter the Conclave, the Cardinals attend the Mass of the Holy Ghost in St. Peter's Basilica. One by one, each takes his place at the confessional. Their aides, the Conclavists, are seated in side pews in formal costume. Each Cardinal is allowed to take two aides into the Conclave; usually he takes one ecclesiastic and one layman. In special cases, after he has obtained the permission of the Sacred College, a Cardinal is allowed a third Conclavist.

A Conclavist cannot be a relative of the Cardinal. If he is a member of a religious order, he cannot be of the same order nor can he be a prelate.

The Basilica is resplendent now. The Dean of the Sacred College appears vested in red chasuble. He walks to the altar at the end of the apsis and the Mass of the Holy Ghost begins. *"Veni, Creator Spiritus, veni Creator Omnium."* ("O come, Holy Ghost, Creator of All Things, help us.")

The Cardinals have all sworn to the Camerlengo to observe all rules concerning the election. From the moment they arrive in Rome they are constantly reminded of their duties and responsibilities. This is not idle suspicion on the part of the Church; the rules stem from its knowledge of human nature and of the importance of the office of Pope.

After the Mass the Cardinals remain seated. When the Dean of the Sacred College who has just officiated at the Mass returns from the Sacristy, a prelate who has been chosen by the Cardinals mounts to the pulpit for an exhortation.* He delivers his sermon in Latin, reminding the Cardinals that the function they are to perform is their greatest privi-

---

* Usually, though not by rule, this task is given to the best Latinist in the Vatican, to the Secretary of Latin Letters.

lege and that they should therefore fix their minds on God and, laying aside personal likes and dislikes, elect a man worthy to become the pastor of the Church. He warns them to act promptly so as not to prolong the Vacancy of the Holy See.

At the end of the sermon, the Cardinals and their aides, in procession, begin to move into the Vatican. At the head of the procession are the Conclavists and the choir. Then comes the papal Cross, followed by the Cardinals accompanied by three to six Masters of Ceremonies and the Secretary of the Sacred College, who always become Secretary of the Conclave. The Cardinals are followed by the officials of the Conclave; by a Capuchin Father, the Confessor of the participants of the Conclave, then two physicians and one surgeon, then the pharmacists with two assistants, the architect of the Conclave, workmen, etc.

The highlight of the procession is, however, the entrance of the Cardinals. Although any male Catholic can be elected Pope, it is assumed that actually the Cardinals will choose the new Pope from the Sacred College. Noting the dignified appearance of the Cardinals in their red robes, spectators may recall that they are called Princes of the Church and, in countries on friendly terms with the Holy See, are received according to protocol and treated like princes of royal blood.

When the Pope creates a Cardinal and places the red hat upon his head, he pronounces the following words: "For the praise of God Almighty, and the ornament of the Holy and Apostolic See, receive the red hat, the special sign of a Cardinal's dignity; by this is signified that even to death and to shedding of blood you should show your courage for the exaltation of Holy Faith, the peace and tranquility of Christian peoples, and the maintenance and increase of the Holy Roman Church."

There have been many instances in Church history in which Cardinals have known suffering and have shed blood. Cardinal Consalvi defied Napoleon and several times was thrown into prison and brought to the very edge of death. Cardinal Faulhauber of Munich and Cardinal Preysing of Berlin risked their lives opposing Hitler. Cardinal Mindszenty of Hungary was sentenced to a life term because of his opposition to a Communist regime. Cardinal Stepinac of Yugoslavia recently served six years in the penitentiary. Cardinal Wyszinski of Poland was arrested by the Communist regime and as this is being written no one knows whether he is dead or alive.

Each of these Cardinals was offered opportunities to escape suffering. Even those who were imprisoned were offered freedom if they would agree to leave their respective countries. None of them accepted.

In the popular imagination, Cardinals are always garbed from head to foot in brilliant red robes. Actually they appear most often in other dress. There are also many misconceptions about the functions of the Cardinals and the reason why they elect the Pope.

The word Cardinal derives from the Latin *cardo,* which means hinge. The Cardinals are the hinges on which swing the doors of the Church.

During the first centuries of Christianity the entire Church was under the administration of the clergy of Rome who acted as helpers and consultants of the Bishop of Rome—i.e., the Pope. In the hierarchy of the Catholic Church a deacon is one with sacred orders, though not a priest. Their function was to care for the material needs of the Church. They also participated in Church administration. With the development of the Papal States and the growth of the Universal Church, the Cardinals were called Cardinal Deacons, Cardinal Priests and Cardinal Bishops to emphasize the fact that the Cardinal Deacons are descendants of the Roman deacons of the first centuries, the Cardinal Priests are descendants of the first pastors of the Roman churches, and the Cardinal Bishops were and still are the chiefs of the dioceses around Rome.

This seemingly senseless tradition has important implications. As has been emphasized, the primary title of the head of the Catholic Church is Bishop of Rome and he becomes Head of the Church because he is Bishop of Rome. The Cardinals gathered in Rome are considered Roman priests electing their Bishop. That is why each Cardinal has a titular church in Rome. When electing the Pope the Cardinals are acting as priests, deacons or Bishops of those churches in Rome which were given to them when they were created Cardinals. According to the rules of the Church, only the Cardinals—that is, the representatives of the clergy of Rome —can elect the Bishop of Rome. Should all the Cardinals ever become extinct, the duty of choosing a Supreme Pastor for the Universal Church would fall, not on the Bishops of the whole world assembled in council, but upon the remaining clergy of the Lateran Basilica of Rome.*

---

* The Lateran Basilica of St. John (and not St. Peter's) is the Cathedral Church of the Bishop of Rome.

Until the Council of Trent in 1545, whenever the Pope appointed a Cardinal he either named a Roman or ordered the new Cardinal to come to Rome and reside there. For example, in the thirteenth century, when several French Bishops were made Cardinals, they had to settle in Rome and the Pope nominated new Bishops in their dioceses. The Council of Trent, however, permitted Cardinals who already were diocesan Bishops, and thus charged with caring for the souls of the faithful, to remain in their own dioceses. But the new practice did not destroy the old rule. A Cardinal appointed by the Pope must have the Pope's permission to keep his diocesan See and no Cardinal who puts foot in Rome may return home without the Pontiff's authorization. Those Cardinals who head the Sacred Congregations and Offices, who are Cardinals of the Roman Curia, may not leave Rome without the permission of the Holy Father.

2. *The Final Preparations*

The procession to the Conclave ends in the Sistine Chapel and silence falls slowly upon the Vatican. Before the Dean of the Sacred College reads the Apostolic Constitution, which governs the Conclave, he once again invokes help by intoning a part of the Mass to the Holy Ghost. *"Oremus; Deus qui corda fidelium . . ."* ("O Lord, who elevated the hearts of the faithful . . .") starts the prayer. Then, the Apostolic Constitution, governing the Conclave and the election, is read by the Dean of the Sacred College. Those parts of the Apostolic Constitution which refer to the period between the death of the Pope and the entrance of the Conclave are left out because this was read to the Cardinals at their arrival in Rome. After having read the Constitution, all Cardinals take an oath, swearing that they will observe the rules contained therein. Then the Dean of the Sacred College addresses them in the form of a brief exhortation, admonishing them to conform to the law.

After a few minutes, the Governor of the Conclave, a high prelate, and the Marshal of the Conclave enter and take oath. The Governors and the Marshals bear greatest responsibility for the independence and integrity of the Conclave, thus they swear alone. Then the rest of the prelates and Conclavists take oath. All take the oath in Latin. The waiters and workers take it in Italian. At this moment, the Dean of the Sacred College gives an order to ring the bells, which means that everyone not belonging to the Conclave must leave at once.

The Conclave is still open, but now the Conclavists go to their rooms and the Prefect of the Masters of Ceremonies with the Architect of the Conclave (the man who designed the small apartments and is responsible for the Conclave's material construction) perform an ancient rite. They go from room to room searching for unauthorized persons, while every ten minutes one of the aides of the Masters of Ceremonies calls loudly: *"Exeunt omnes."* ("Everybody [who does not belong to the Conclave] should leave.")

The search continues for more than an hour. Drawers are opened, draperies pulled aside, dark corners lighted. After having searched the entire Conclave, they remain and wait at the only entrance which has not been walled off.

Meanwhile, in the Sistine Chapel, the Cardinals proceed

to identify the Conclavists. Each of them shows his credentials and is identified as belonging to one or another Cardinal and told which room is assigned to him.

The closing (i.e., locking) of the Conclave takes place at the entrance of the Scala Pio Nono (Pius IX Stairway) which is the wide and large stairway leading from the Bronze Gate (Portone di Bronzo) of the Vatican, up to the St. Damasus Courtyard.

When everybody who does not belong there has left the territory of the Conclave, the members of the Noble Guard leave also. The Noble Guard is the bodyguard of the Pope. Its function is suspended after the Pope is buried. There is one exception, however. At the entrance procession into the Conclave, the Cardinals are accompanied by Noble Guardists, because each Cardinal is considered a Prince Hereditary, a potential Pope. No one knows which of them will emerge as Supreme Pontiff, thus every one of them is entitled to the honor of being accompanied while he enters the Conclave.

The Marshal of the Conclave and his aides stand outside. The Governor of the Conclave and the Masters of Ceremonies stay inside. They close the door together and the Marshal from the outside turns the key. A few moments later, on the inside, the Governor of the Conclave's key also turns in the lock. At this moment, the Marshal of the Conclave orders his flag hoisted on the Vatican palace and at the Conclave's entrance.

For many hundreds of years, the flag bore the coat of arms of the Chigi family. Since Prince Chigi-Albani, who was Marshal of a Conclave in 1939, died, no one has been appointed to this post. Of course, there is no rule that only a member of the Chigi family could become Marshal of the Conclave. For hundreds of years, this was kept as a tradition. But, it is conceivable that anyone Roman, even unknown, could become the holder of this important function. Since the flag is hoisted, the Marshal is responsible for the integrity of the Conclave. No one can give him orders. No Cardinal can tell him to open the doors until the Pope is duly chosen. No secular sovereign or force can direct him to permit any act of intrusion and if one did, the Marshal and his men would defend themselves and the Conclave, if necessary with their lives. The entire Catholic world will obey the Pope who will be chosen, but its loyalty will be given only to one chosen in a strictly secret election.

The Conclave takes place in more than two hundred rooms, because the apartments of the Cardinals alone number seventy—and these apartments have at least three rooms, one belonging to the Cardinal, and two to his Conclavists.

Doors and other entrances of the territory which serves for the Conclave have been walled up. Windows through which someone might signal or smuggle a message have been sealed and painted with opaque paint.

In the past, there have been serious as well as minor breaches of secrecy. During the Conclave of 1724, one of the Cardinals also held the post of Ambassador of Charles VI to the Holy See. The Emperor wished to let the Cardinal, inside the Conclave, know which candidates were not to his liking and the written message was delivered to him by an agile young officer who climbed the walls by using the iron bars of windows as a ladder. When he was unable to reach the window through which he had planned to hand the letter to the waiting Cardinal, he impaled the message on his sword and in that fashion raised it.

During the election of Pius X in 1903, before the result could be announced, an employee of the Conclave appeared at one of the windows facing the Piazza. He held a big pair of scissors in his hand and imitated the gesture of a tailor cutting cloth. Everyone knew what he meant: the name of the Patriarch of Venice was Giuseppe Sarto and *sarto* in Italian means tailor. Cardinal Sarto was the new Pope.

There are three rotating openings through which food can be delivered to the Conclave, but they are not large enough so that anyone could be smuggled in or out. Moreover, they are watched day and night by the special guard of the Marshal of the Conclave.

Newspapers and magazines can be sent in only through this censorship and under no circumstances may a Cardinal or a Conclavist send out any book, newspaper or magazine. The Cardinals and their aides and servants are permitted to write letters, but the letters must go through one of the rotating openings and be censored.

No Cardinal or Conclavist is allowed to use the telephone. If there is urgent need for its use, the text of the message must be submitted for censorship and, if approved, a third person makes the call.

The Vatican switchboard is under strict control; few lines are used and those few under the Marshal's supervision. The Marshal is assisted by a group of Church dignitaries and the police work is done by the Swiss Guard and the gendarmes of the Vatican.

Though the Cardinals and Conclavists are no longer forced to live in one room, the accommodations for them are not spacious. Carpenters, masons and electricians, who have been working in the Conclave area since the death of the Pope, have subdivided the large rooms, some of which are sixty feet square. Each Cardinal receives a bed-sitting room, with bathroom. The apartments are furnished with simple beds, chests of drawers, desks and chairs.

Since there are more than three hundred persons in the Conclave, there are many problems of maintenance. Workmen have built a large and modern electric kitchen and pantry, with refrigerators, cooking utensils and so on, and there all meals are prepared. Until 1878, the Cardinals received their meals from the kitchens of their own palaces and twice a day the people of Rome would watch a parade of food-bearing *dapieri,* the colorful coaches, with coachmen and four servants in different uniforms, according to the Cardinals' nationality and rank.

Vatican City has all the facilities needed to supply the Conclave with necessities. It has its own underground storerooms, its own power plant and emergency plants, its own oil tanks and cellars for hundreds of tons of coal, and modern workshops for all kinds of repairs.

The caves of the Vatican, concerning which there have been many uninformed and malicious rumors, are full of other goods than jewels—with shoes, candles and textiles, for example. It was from them that Pope Pius XII sent supplies to help stricken sections in Germany, Italy and other countries.

Near Rome, at Castel Gandolfo, a modern farm belonging

to the Holy See provides milk, vegetables, meat, olive oil and fats. Vatican City has its own emergency wells for drinking water. In fact, all Rome drinks the water of the popes, for it was they who modernized the Roman aqueducts, and the great fountains in Rome that visitors admire are not the products of pompous imaginations but monuments commemorating the termination of new sections of aqueduct for the Roman people.

Thus all is ready for the Conclave. There are even a small pharmacy, a small hospital and a large modern doctor's office prepared to undertake minor operations.

3. *The Election Itself*

The center of the Conclave, the Sistine Chapel, now comes splendidly to life. It was constructed by Pope Sixtus IV (hence the name Sistine Chapel) in 1473. Sixtus employed the greatest artists of the age, from Botticelli to Ghirlandaio and from Mino da Fiesole to Signorelli. It was his successors, Julius II and Paul III, who commissioned Michelangelo to do the gigantic frescoes of the Last Judgment.

The chapel, as large as an ordinary church, is transformed for the occasion. The altar is covered with a tapestry representing the descent of the Holy Ghost upon the Apostles. Above it hangs a violet baldachino or canopy with a red border edged with gold. Along the walls are the thrones of the Cardinals, the electors, and before each throne is a small table bearing the Cardinal's name in Latin and his coat of arms. In the center of the chapel are four larger tables on which the votes are counted. All the furniture is covered with purple cloth.

Before the altar is a large table on which are a paten and a chalice. When a Cardinal casts a vote, the ballot is first placed on the paten, then put into the chalice which serves as ballot box. Near this table is the famous stove, its chimney leading out through a window facing St. Peter's Square. In the stove, when the voting has been inconclusive, the ballots are burnt with damp straw, producing the traditional black smoke indicating that the Church is still without a Pope. When the choice is finally made, the ballots are burned without straw and white smoke informs the outside world that a Pope has been elected.

All those in the Conclave feel the burden of history. Today the interior of the Vatican has been modernized and the thick walls of the buildings are mere curiosities. There are walls sixteen feet thick with staircases built into them. Before the election of Leo IV, the Saracens pillaged Rome and carried off a massive silver altar which had been donated by Constantine. In 848 Leo IV asked the Christian Kings of Europe for contributions to fortify the city and he carried out the gigantic task in two years. When the Saracens landed again they found the city and the Vatican Palace defended. The fortified walls were blessed by Leo IV with the words "May no enemy of Christ, of the Church or St. Peter ever pass these gates." The fortifications ran about five miles around the whole city, protecting the churches and the inhabitants, then numbering about five thousand. These same ninth century walls bound the modern State of the Vatican City and are in themselves enough to create awe in all those charged with the duty of electing another in the long line of popes.

And now inside the Conclave, there is one more step to be taken. The credentials of the Conclavists already have been checked several times, but now they are checked again.

Invited individually into the Sistine Chapel, the Conclavists are identified by the Secretary of the Conclave and by three Cardinals. Thereafter they are free to walk around or to rest in their rooms. No rule restricts the Conclavists or Cardinals from talking to one another, but there is no election campaign among the Conclavists for one or another Cardinal; the Conclavist has no opinion on the best man to elect, or if he has he keeps it to himself.

The Cardinals do not talk about the election with their aides in terms that could be considered propaganda for one of the electors and there are no special meetings of Cardinals to discuss the possibilities. The Cardinals may talk to one another individually but outside the Sistine Chapel, where all electoral meetings take place, there are no official or semi-official functions.

Though the election is secret we know in what form it takes place. The Apostolic Constitution of Pius XII recognizes the validity of three methods of electing a Pope: inspiration, compromise and balloting. It is election by inspiration when, on the first day, the Cardinal-electors unanimously proclaim one name without proceeding to a vote. Compromise may occur in extraordinary circumstances. In that case the Cardinals entrust the choice to no less than three and no more than seven of their number. They must be selected unanimously and receive full instructions for the election from the Sacred College. The Cardinals bind themselves in advance to accept the choice of the selected group.

The third method of election, by ballot, is the method usually followed. Pius XII, his predecessor and all popes of the eighteenth and nineteenth centuries were elected by secret ballot.

All popes since Urban VI, elected in 1378, have been Cardinals and all since Adrian VI of Utrecht, chosen in 1522, have been Italians.

Election is now by two-thirds majority plus one because the law invalidates any ballot cast by an elector for himself. When only a two-thirds majority was required, a complicated system was necessary to identify the ballot of the Cardinal elected by just the required majority in order to determine if he voted for himself.

On the morning of the first day of the Conclave, Cardinals and Conclavists participate at Mass. Then the Conclavists leave and the Master of Ceremonies and the Secretary of the Sacred College present the ballots to the Cardinals, who previously have taken their seats on their thrones. The ballot is a three-by-three-inch slip divided into two equal parts. On the upper part in Latin are the following words: "I choose as Sovereign Pontiff ——" On the lower part are the words: "His Eminence Cardinal ——"

Having distributed the ballots, the Master of Ceremonies leaves the chapel and the last in rank of the Cardinal Deacons closes the door behind him, leaving only Cardinals in the chapel during the balloting. Usually they have about half an hour to name their choice.

Cardinals who are ill and who remain in their rooms vote in the following way: Three Cardinals take a box with an opening large enough to permit the insertion of a folded ballot and, in the presence of all the Cardinals, open it, certify that it is empty, then lock it and leave the key on the altar. Thereupon, with blank ballots, they proceed to the rooms of the Cardinals who are ill and these mark their ballots in the usual fashion. If a Cardinal is too weak to write, he may be assisted by an ecclesiastic of his choice who is bound to secrecy under pain of automatic excommunication.

Now the three Cardinals return and, in the presence of all the Cardinals, open the box, count the ballots and place them first on the paten and then in the chalice.

Cardinals who vote in the Sistine Chapel, having filled out their ballots, rise in the order of seniority. Ballot between thumb and index finger, each Cardinal elevates his hand and carries his ballot to the altar. He places the ballot on the paten, then drops it into the chalice and returns to his seat, having first pronounced the following oath: "I take to witness Christ Our Lord who is Judge to me that I hereby vote for him who, before God, I feel should be elected."

Since the election is secret, one can only surmise what motivates a Cardinal's choice. Generally speaking, he will vote for the man he considers the most able and worthy in the College of Cardinals despite the fact that, according to Catholic belief, the Pope's most important pronouncements and actions are guided by the Holy Ghost.

The rules of the Conclave indicate that an elector should not be guided by secular influences and obviously a man is unsuited to be Supreme Shepherd of all races and classes if he has specialized political commitments.

In general, the Pope should be physically able, though

there have been times when the Cardinals have voted for the quiet, mellow wisdom that ideally comes with old age. A year before his death at ninety-four, Pope Leo XIII (1878–1903) after a serious illness received a Spanish nobleman who expressed his good wishes by saying: "May God let you live a hundred years, Your Holiness." Leo smiled and answered jokingly: "My dear son, why do you want to set limits to God's power and grace?"

On the other hand, when Pius XI was elected in 1922 the postwar world situation was so complicated that it called for a Pontiff not only of erudition but of strong physique, endurance and determination. Cardinal Ratti, later Pius XI, was such a man, a well-known mountain climber, active and dynamic, and he became one of the great popes.

When Pius XII was elected in 1939 the world was threatened with a new war, and it is notable that the Cardinals did not hesitate to break the unwritten rule that no Secretary of State of the Vatican should be elected Pope. They gave their votes to Cardinal Pacelli, later Pius XII, who from early youth had been a diplomat, who had visited and was well known in much of the western world, and who all his life had worked hard and brilliantly for peace.

At times, again, knowledge of worldly affairs may be considered a liability rather than an asset in a potential Pope. When Cardinal Sarto, who became Pius X, was chosen there were many attempts at outside interference with the Papacy. There was little danger that Cardinal Sarto would become involved in secular politics for he was totally uninterested in such matters. In this instance, the Cardinals apparently decided that the Church needed as head a very simple, saintly priest.

Ideally, the man chosen as Pope should have proved himself both a good priest and a good executive. Two attributes of a good priest are an exemplary private life and dedication to his flock. A good executive is one who has kept his house (in this case his diocese) in order. It is reasonable to assume that he will keep the Holy See in order as well.

As the Church grew in importance because the Emperor Constantine saw political advantage in favoring the Christian faith the Papacy began to take the form in which it exists today. Says Thomas B. Morgan in his book *The Listening Post* (G. P. Putnam & Sons, New York, 1944): "A union started which established Christianity as a part of the Imperial system. The Roman pagans had always identified religion and the priesthood with the state. Roman organization and Christian faith were joined. This merger permitted the new cult to profit by the efficient administration the Empire had built up. . . . The Christian Church grew into a vast organization. It had a hierarchical form copied to a great extent from the Roman practice all over the world. Metropolitan heads, archbishops, bishops, patriarchs and primates were created, with the regular gradation of subordinate orders of priests, deacons and other clerics who were able to administer far-off regions and cities." The advantage of having an efficient executive at the head of this far-flung organization is obvious.

As the Church gained official status within the Empire, the Papacy often became a target for adventurers. There were times when it was in the hands of those whose aim was secular, times when power-hungry individuals got hold of it, times when it passed from one rich Roman family to another.

This had less effect on the faithful than might be supposed, partly because, while Catholics believe that their Church is of divine origin, they recognize that the Pope is human and that no man is without sin. Again, in the Papacy the bad has invariably been overcome and overshadowed by the good. The faithful themselves have often seen to that, as they did when after the scandals of the tenth century they demanded the election of the monk Hildebrand. In general they exert pressure indirectly, not as they would in a democratic society, through direct ballot, but through their Bishops, priests and leading laymen who have the courage to speak out.

Since 1917 it has been a rule that only priests can become Cardinals. This has tended to improve the spiritual quality of papal elections. In early times the office of Cardinal, having been administrative originally, did not require consecration. Cardinal Secretary of State Antonelli, for example, was a layman; he was the foreign minister of Pius IX (1846–1878) and a most able diplomat.

The will to elect the best to the Papacy has always been kept alive, sometimes by some of the Cardinal-electors and sometimes by all. For example, there is not much doubt that St. Gregory the Great (590–604) was elected not only because he had a brilliant executive mind but because he was humble and deeply religious. Gregory was the first Pope to sign himself *Servant of the Servants of God.*

Again, in 1585, when the Conclave was seemingly ruled by two factions, the Farnese and the Medici families, none of their candidates was elected. Instead a Franciscan monk, apparently in very poor health, was chosen. And Felice Peretti, the Franciscan, did not belong to either of the two great families or even to an ordinary family. In his youth he had been a swineherd.

At the Conclave of 1846 no outside power was able to influence the election, though some tried. Austria served notice that it would veto the election if Cardinal Mastai Ferretti were chosen. He was chosen nevertheless.

Mastai Ferretti was one of the scrutators, the Cardinals who count the votes. His duty was to read aloud the names that appeared on the ballots. Full of emotion, he read his own name again and again and out of modesty asked to be relieved of the scrutator's duties. This, however, would have invalidated the election, and consequently he—Pius IX—became the first Pope to announce his own choice.

Procedures at the opening and counting of the votes are rarely so dramatic, though they are always highly formal. First the number of ballots is counted. The senior Cardinal scrutator covers the chalice with the paten and shakes it. If the number of the ballots does not correspond with the number of Cardinals, the ballots are not opened but immediately burned and a new vote gets under way.

If the number of ballots is the same as the number of Cardinals, the ballots are opened and the votes are tabulated. The first Cardinal scrutator opens a ballot, looks at the name on it, and without a word passes it to the second scrutator, who also examines the name and hands the ballot to a third scrutator. The third scrutator then calls the name out loudly, so that each Cardinal may hear it and record it on a printed sheet bearing the names of all Cardinals present. The announcing scrutator marks the vote on his own sheet also.

When the count is over, a scrutator announces the number of votes cast for each Cardinal. If no Cardinal has received two-thirds plus one, there must be further balloting. At the end of each balloting process, the last in rank of the Cardinal scrutators passes a needle through the center of each ballot, strings all the ballots on a thread, knots the thread and places the string of ballots in a special chalice on a special table. After the tallying by the scrutators has been checked to insure accuracy, the ballots are burned before the assembled Cardinals with the assistance of the Master of Ceremonies.

The Cardinals vote twice in the morning, twice in the afternoon. Morning or afternoon, the ballots are burned after the second vote. When white smoke finally appears the world does not yet know who has been elected. The telephones still do not work from inside the Conclave. And Pius XII prohibited the use of telegraphic senders and receivers as well as radio inside the Conclave. No pictures from inside the locked Conclave will ever appear, because no cameras of any sort are allowed.

When the ballot count shows that a new Pope has been chosen, all the Cardinals in the chapel stand but remain at their thrones.

The next steps are rigidly ceremonial. The Cardinal Deacon last in rank sounds a bell and opens the chapel door. The Secretary of the Conclave enters, with the Master of Ceremonies and the Sacristan of the Vatican. Now the Dean of the Sacred College of Cardinals, the Cardinal Camerlengo and the three prelates who have just entered proceed to the

Cardinal who received the requisite majority. The Dean asks loudly in Latin: *"Acciptasne electionem?"* ("Do you accept the result of the election?")

For the chosen person, this is the most dramatic moment of life.

In his Constitution, Pius XII begs his successors to accept the honor and not to be frightened by it. For the chosen Cardinal there is only acceptance or rejection. He cannot ask for time; he must decide right there at that very moment while the Dean of the Sacred College awaits his answer.

Slowly he utters the Latin word: *"Accepto."* ("I accept.") From this instant, he has supreme jurisdiction.

The clear and straightforward answer of the elected is extremely important because this acceptance makes the election effective. It is remembered that one of the modern popes, when asked whether he accepted the election, answered saying that he accepted it because it was the will of God and he thus resigned himself to His will. The Dean of the Sacred College, however, was not content with the answer and asked the elected Cardinal respectfully but firmly to answer with an expression which unequivocally signified total acceptance of the election.

Without delay, each Cardinal pulls a string on the side of his throne which lowers the canopy above it. Only the canopy on the throne of the new Pope remains open, symbolizing the fact that the Cardinals are no longer his equals. His reign will date from the day of his Coronation but from this moment on he has all the rights a Pope possesses.

The Dean of the Sacred College has another question to

ask: *"Quo modo vis vocari?"* ("What name do you choose for yourself?"). Since the eleventh century, few popes have kept their baptismal names. After a new Pope announces his new name, he proceeds to the altar and kneels in brief prayer. Then, followed by the Master of Ceremonies, the Sacristan and the Secretary of the Conclave, he retires into the Sacristy. Before the Pope is clothed in his new vestments, the Secretary of the Conclave approaches him, kneels and offers him the white skullcap called the zucchetto.

Until recently it was customary for the Pope to remove his own cap, the red one of a Cardinal, and put it on the head of the Secretary of the Conclave, which means that he will become a Cardinal. At any rate, most popes have followed this custom. At the election of Leo XIII in 1878, however, the absent-minded Pope put his own zucchetto in his pocket. A few weeks later he corrected his "error" by making the forgotten secretary a Cardinal.

At Leo's death, the question of the cap came up again. While the Pope lay dying, the prospective Secretary of the Conclave died—just a few hours before the death of the Pope himself. The College of Cardinals had no right to appoint a new Secretary, but the problem was solved by the creation of the position of Prosecretary to which was named the highly respected, versatile young Bishop Merry del Val. The new Pope, Pius X, did not forget to put the red zucchetto on the Bishop's head, and in a few days made him Secretary of State. It must be kept in mind that this was not and is not a rule.

4. *Ceremonies Following the Election*

The morning after the Conclave assembles, the Piazza is thronged with tens of thousands of spectators. People climb to the top of the colonnade and the Palatine Guard is hard pressed to hold a line about fifty yards from the Basilica's façade. According to the Lateran Treaty, the Piazza is Vatican territory and usually papal gendarmes are posted at the entrance of the Via Conciliazione. This morning, however, there are no gendarmes and people flow like rivers converging on the Piazza from all sides. Soon the connecting streets as well as the Square are filled. Traffic is diverted as time passes. By nine o'clock about five hundred thousand people are assembled, with all eyes directed toward one point. Those who are close enough may see the small black bent chimney emerging from one of the Sistine Chapel's windows.

If the election lasts more than one day, this scene on the Piazza will be repeated daily until the smoke is white.

In the Sacristy of the Sistine Chapel robes have been prepared. There the Sacristan and the Secretary of the Conclave assist the Pope in donning the white silk cassock, the pectoral cross, the purple silk slippers embroidered with gold crosses, a red mantle trimmed with ermine and a gold-embroidered white stole.

Thus vested, the Pope returns to the altar and occupies the small throne which was waiting for him during the election. He then stands and imparts his first pontifical Blessing to the members of the Sacred College who elected him.

When he is again seated, one by one, according to seniority, the Cardinals approach him, kneel and kiss his hands.

After this ceremony the Cardinal Camerlengo, accompanied by the Master of Ceremonies, genuflects and puts the Fisherman's Ring on the Pope's finger. The ring has no seal; the seal, it will be recalled, was destroyed at the death of the Pope's predecessor. The new Pope therefore removes the ring and returns it to the Master of Ceremonies who will obtain a new seal bearing the new Pope's name.

Now the Pontiff receives the so-called second obedience of the Cardinals. While he is still seated on his throne in the chapel, they again approach him and, genuflecting, kiss his feet, then kiss the hands through the mantle which covers them. Then the Pope and each Cardinal embrace, first from the right and then from the left. The ceremony signifies that the cardinals, no longer equals, are bound to obey.

In the meantime, the first Cardinal Deacon appears on the balcony of St. Peter's Church. The multitude of hundreds of thousands falls silent. They know that the new Pope has been elected because they have seen the white smoke.

The Cardinal lifts his right hand indicating that he will start to speak.

"Annuntio vobis gaudium magnum; habemus Papam." ("I announce to you a great joy; we have a new Pope.")

The Cardinal stops for a moment, then continues: *"Eminentissimum ac Reverendissimum Dominum Cardinalem . . . qui sibi nomen . . . imposuit."* ("His Eminence the Most Reverend Lord Cardinal . . . who choose the following name . . .")

His last words are drowned by the cheers of the crowd and in a few seconds the news is known in all corners of the world.

From inside the Sistine Chapel the Pope, now rising from his throne, walks to the same balcony. On the way he imparts his Blessing. Then suddenly he is on the balcony facing Rome. Joyfully the city greets its new Bishop. He faces the multitude and beyond them the world and raises a hand in Benediction.

One hundred and five of the 362 popes have been Romans, seventy-seven others Italians, fifteen Frenchmen, fourteen Greeks, seven Syrians, four Tuscans, four Germans, three Spaniards, two Africans, two Dalmatians, two Lombards, two Sardinians. There have been one Alsatian, one Burgundian, one Calabrian-Greek, one Dutch, one Englishman, one Lorrainer, one Austrogoth, one Samnite (or Sabine), three Sicilians, one Umbrian, and one—St. Peter—Galilean Jew. Forty-one have belonged to religious orders, including twenty-five Benedictines, five Franciscans, four Dominicans and three Cistercians. Seventy-seven are venerated as saints and seven have been beatified.

The title Pope comes from the Greek and means father. It has been in use since the eleventh century. The new Pope will sign his utterances *Papa* as well as *Servus Servorum Dei* (Servant of the Servants of God).

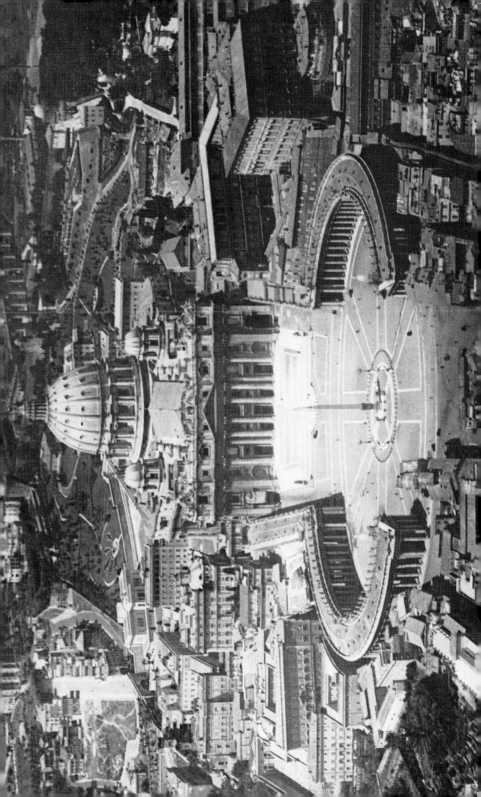

*The bronze door of the Vatican Palace is closed im-
mediately after a Pope's death. Only the small entrance, manned by a Swiss Guard, remains open.*

*After the death of a Pope, the flags of the Vatican
fly at half-mast.*

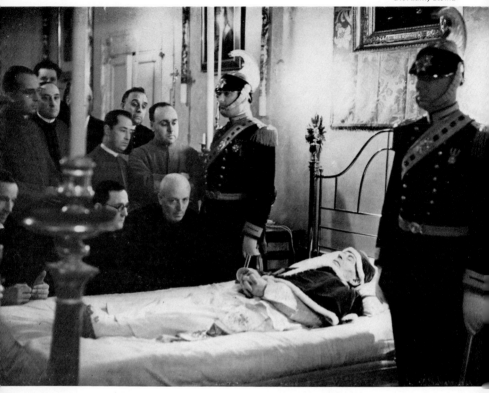

A Pope (Pius XI) lies on his deathbed. The kneeling priests are Penitentiaries of St. Peter's Basilica. The uniformed men are members of the Noble Guard.

During the Vacancy of the Holy See, the deceased Pope's body is transported first to the Sistine Chapel (below) and then to St. Peter's Church.

On the way to St. Peter's Church the body of the Pope is carried by the Noble Guard. The soldiers with halberds are Swiss Guards. The priests with candles are Penitentiaries of St. Peter's.

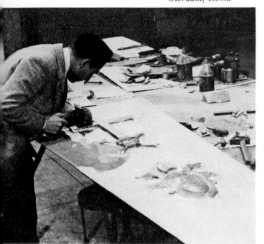

At St. Peter's Church, the Pontiff's body is placed in these coffins. Two are of wood, cyprus and elm (below) and one of lead.

The lead coffin—this is its cover— will be sealed with the seals of the Camerlengo and the Major-domo.

The Chapel of the Most Holy Sacrament within St.
Peter's Basilica, where the body of the Pope lies after
being brought from the Sistine Chapel.

The photograph below is o
of the catafalque (coffin wit
out a body), taken during t
Novemdiali, the nine d
series of Requiem Masses
St. Peter's Basilica.

In the three coffins, the remains of the Pope
are lowered into the grotto of St. Peter's
Basilica, behind the main altar.

This is the entrance to St. Peter's Tomb in the underground grotto of St. Peter's Basilica.

...IMA FVGIFE[
VALERIAE MAXIMAE COIVGI E[
OLYMPIANO FILIO ETSVIS   LIBERTIS
TABVSQVE POSTERISQ EORVM

4

*The huge portico of St. Peter's Square. Right: entrances to the
Church.*

*A detail from the entrance to St. Peter's Tomb.
It lies under the Basilica's main altar.*

Giordani, Roma

The bedroom above is for memb
of the Noble Guard who are
mitted to the Conclave.

Entrances to the Conclave are wal
shut, all except one which is secur
locked and guarded.

Giordani, Roma

*To insure secrecy, windows of the Conclave are covered with opaque
paint.*

In preparation for the Conclave, a dining table is set up in th
Sala dei Arazzi.

oes are fashioned for the new
ntiff. Note the cross on the in-
p.

Cassocks of different sizes are readied
for the election of a new Pope.

These sleeping quarters in the Conclave will be occupied by Cardinal.

Medals and coins issued during the Vacancy of the Holy See. Top Commemorative medal of the Cardinal Camerlengo. Center: Com memorative medal of the Governor of the Conclave. Bottom: Five an ten lire coins issued by the Vatican during the Vacancy. Bottom, cente Reverse side of the coins with the Camerlengo's coat of arms.

'he Sistine Chapel is prepared for the Conclave. On both sides are
₁e thrones of the Cardinals.

G. Felici, Roma

One of the Conclave's small revolving doors. It is guarded by the Monsignor of the Apostolic Chamber (center), a Swiss Guard (left) and a uniformed Papal Gendarme.

The sealing machine of the Holy See is prepared so that documents may be sealed after the new Pope is elected.

The two chalices and the paten used in the Conclave in the process of voting.

All the canopies over the Cardinal's thrones, except that over Cardinal elected Pope, are lowered and the thrones are removed.

G. Felici, Roma

Below (right) in the Sistine Chapel is the famous stove in which the ballots are burned. The sack (center) contains straw.

This was the ballot used during the last Conclave.

White smoke issuing from the chimney of the stove in the Sistine Chapel means that a Pope has been elected.

Outside the Conclave, in temporary booths in St. Peter's Square, journalists telephone the news that a Pope has been chosen.

Seated on his Sedia Gestatoria, or portable throne, the newly elected Pope is carried to St. Peter's Basilica for his Coronation

At the main altar of St. Peter's Basilica, the new Pope and attendants (left) celebrate a Solemn Mass on his Coronation Day.

*Four tiaras in the Vatican treasury. The third from the left is the rea
one. The others are of little or no value.*

Giordani, Rom

*This, the actual crowning, is the climax of the Coronation cele-
bration. It takes place on the center balcony of St. Peter's Church.*

The Palatine Guard, shown in dress uniform, has five hundred members, charged with general guard service during ceremonies.

Below: Papal Gendarmes, in full dress. Papal guards, who now serve chiefly as symbols, once actually fought battles.

These are some of the two hundred members of the Papal Noble Guard, all of whom belong to the Italian nobility.

These men are Bussolanti *wth their chief (third from the left).*

In a Vatican courtyard, a recruit is sworn into the Swiss Guards. Their first two hundred members arrived in Rome in 1506.

Crowds pack the top of the Colonnade and the roofs of nearby buildings on Coronation Day.

This is St. Peter's Square, crowded to capacity, at the moment of the Coronation.

Giordani, Roma

CHAPTER IV

The Coronation

1. *The Crown of the Pope*

FROM times immemorial men and women have been crowned to honor them, to put them at the head of groups or nations, to emphasize that they are persons set apart. There have been crowns of flowers, of iron, of bronze and silver and gold and there was once a crown of thorns—a mock Coronation of Christ to ridicule His Kingdom which is not of this earth. In the minds and hearts of the faithful the mock ceremony became the greatest of all time and the crowned Person, with bleeding head, was indeed and remained a chosen one, the chosen Son of God.

In all ages, almost every country under monarchical government has had Coronation ceremonies with features peculiar to its own traditions. To the person crowned the ceremony has always been a reminder of his special rights and duties. Receiving the obedience of his people, he in turn

[97]

has solemnly sworn to obey God by whose grace he has been elevated.

Constantine the Great wore a diadem most of his life and was buried with it. When Julian was proclaimed Emperor in A.D. 360, soldiers hoisted him high, standing upon a shield, and the standard-bearer took off his necklace and put it on the new Emperor's head. As Christianity became more and more an integral part of the Roman Empire, the ceremony of Coronation became more and more a sacramental act in which the person of the King was blessed and anointed. Similarly, in England, France, Spain and many other countries the Coronation became rooted in Church doctrine. The chosen one was anointed and blessed in the name of God.

When Queen Elizabeth of England was crowned in 1953, many Catholics recognized the ceremonies as part of the Coronation of a Pope.

The Coronation of a Pope is, of course, religious from beginning to end. It is a long series of beautifully and solemnly arranged prayers centered around the highest function that any Catholic ecclesiastic can perform: the celebration of the sacrifice of the Mass.

In a papal Coronation, the historical details, the uniforms, the hymns, and the act of Coronation itself are only reminders. They are symbols whose meaning can best be described in the first three words of the hymn that greets the new Pope when, in solemn procession, he enters the portico of St. Peter's Church: "*Tu es Petrus. . . .*" ("You are Peter") —the successor of Peter the Fisherman.

A new Pope takes no elaborate oath. He utters one Latin word after he is notified that he has been elected: "*Accepto.*"

He makes no proclamation and no Coronation is necessary to establish his powers or position. As a matter of fact, popes were not crowned during the first ten centuries.

The papal Coronation grew out of ceremonies connected with the consecration of a Bishop. The first successors of St. Peter were elected Bishops. Until about the tenth century all the popes were laymen or priests and had to be consecrated before receiving the plenitude of their powers. How the first consecrations were performed we do not know, but from approximately the fifth century a distinctive covering was placed on the head of the new Bishop of Rome during the Consecration ceremony.

A Bishop's crown was a round, bulbous hat made of cloth of camel hair (that is why it is sometimes called a *camelaucium*). This hat, worn by all the Bishops including the Pope, took different forms in different regions. In the western world it evolved to the form known as the mitre. In certain parts of the East, real crowns were worn as they might be worn by royalty. From the tenth century on, popes received two "crowns," the Bishop's mitre and, during their Coronation as popes, the tiara.

By the first half of the twelfth century, a papal crown was a velvet hat with one metal crown. During the rule of Boniface VIII (1294–1303) a second and third crown were added. The three crowns are decorated with precious stones and are sometimes said to symbolize the teaching, ruling and sanctifying church. There is no unique opinion as to what the three crowns originally meant. When the Dean of the Sacred College puts the tiara upon the head of the Pope in the Coronation formula, he says that the Pope should remember being 1) Father of the Princes of Kings, 2) Pontiff of the World and 3) Vicar of Our Saviour Jesus Christ on this Earth.

As the Papacy grew in importance, new tiaras were created by the jewelers of the Holy See or were donated by rulers loyal to the Pope. At one time there were nine tiaras in the Treasury of the Vatican, all of them extremely valuable because of their precious stones and artistic design. All were carried off by the armies of Bonaparte.

Pius VII (1800–1823) had no tiara to be crowned with; his three crowns were cut from gilded paper, a sign that the material worth of the crown is unimportant. When Pius VII signed a concordat with Napoleon, the Emperor presented a new and precious tiara to him. During the pontificate of Pius IX, when the armies of the Italian unification movement closed in on Rome, the Pope had a worthless copy of Napoleon's tiara made and the original was hidden to save it from looters.

Today, the Vatican possesses the following tiaras: 1) one donated by Napoleon, 2) one made by Pius IX, 3) a tiara that Leo XIII received as a gift, and 4) one Pius XI received in 1922 after his election from the people of Milan.

In early times, the papal Coronation took place in the Lateran Basilica. In the sixteenth century it was moved to the large balcony of St. Peter's Church. After 1870, because of the hostility of the Italian Government of that time, it was performed inside St. Peter's until the Coronation of Pius XII in 1939 which again occurred on the balcony of St. Peter's Basilica.

During the Middle Ages, when the Pope was a secular as

well as spiritual ruler, the head of large areas of the Italian peninsula, the Coronation was even more impressive than it is today. Later, especially during the eighteenth century, a papal Coronation was often the occasion for the greatest popular festival of the city of Rome.

The highlight of these long-past Coronations from a popular point of view was the *cavalcate papale,* the papal calvacade, in which the Pope, after being crowned, rode, accompanied by his entire court and by detachments of the pontifical armies, from the Vatican to the Lateran Basilica to take possession of his official church. In these cavalcades the papal court, the Roman nobility and the pontifical armies spared no pains or expense to emphasize the importance of the event.

All Cardinals and members of the nobility, all foreign delegations were accompanied by special guards and servants in multicolored uniforms and bearing elaborately designed banners. Drums, trumpets and fanfares sounded, alternating with the slow Gregorian chants of the clergy and the prayers of members of the mendicant orders whose poor habits were in sharp contrast to the magnificence of the procession. The papal cavalcade was a slowly flowing, streetwide river of gold and silver, of scarlet velvet and silk brocade.

2. *The Papal Guards and the Decoration of St. Peter's*

Reduced in size today, the Coronation is still the greatest and best organized ceremony in the world. There is no papal cavalcade with prancing Arab horses and the papal procession, which starts in the Vatican Palace, ends in St. Peter's

Basilica, but the Church has kept almost everything in the ceremonies that is meaningful and dignified, serving to remind the faithful and the world in general of the importance of the Pope and the Papacy.

The Coronation is divided into the following parts: the formation of the procession within the Vatican Palace; the vesting of the Pope for the papal Mass; the procession into the portico of St. Peter's Basilica where the sacred ceremonies are performed; the procession into the Basilica to the Chapel of the Holy Sacrament for adoration of the Eucharist; the procession into St. Peter's Chapel of St. Gregory and the vesting of the Cardinals; the procession to the papal altar and the preparation for the Mass; the "praising of the Pope"; the papal Mass, with its distinctive details; the placing of the sacred pallium upon the Pope's shoulders: the procession after the Mass to the balcony of St. Peter's Basilica; the Coronation of the Pope in the open air before the eyes of the multitude.

Only during a Coronation is one fully aware of the gigantic proportions of St. Peter's Basilica. The maintenance of this great church is the function of an organization called Rev. Fabbrica di San Pietro (Venerable Edifice of St. Peter's), a workshop whose employees are architects, sculptors, masons, carpenters and electricians. They work under the direction of a high-ranking prelate and are well versed in history, art and liturgy. The workmen in the Basilica are called Sanpietrini (the people of St. Peter's) and it is an honor to be made one of them. There are families who have had sons among the Sanpietrini for generations.

It is a huge task to decorate St. Peter's for the Coronation.

An army of Sanpietrini sets to work almost at the moment when the white smoke of the Sistine Chapel's stove announces that a new Pope has been elected.

Those who will be allowed in the Basilica during the Coronation receive earliest consideration. To each of these the Secretary of State of the Vatican issues an ornate invitation telling him how he should be dressed and what place in the church he will occupy. Some spots are considered more, some less desirable, depending on their closeness to the ceremonies.

On the right and left sides of the apsis, benches covered with red cloth serve for Cardinals and Bishops. Behind them are seats for the most distinguished guests, including special representatives of foreign governments and the diplomatic corps accredited to the Vatican. About five thousand of the seventy-five or eighty thousand guests in the Basilica will be seated.

The floor of the route of the papal procession is covered with red carpet. The pillars of the Basilica and many sections of the walls support heavy embroidered brocade. The hundred and sixty altars, mostly of marble, bloom with flowers. On them shine thousands of wax candles and candles with electric bulbs. There are endless chains of lights around the inside of the Basilica's dome and powerful floodlights point to the side chapels. Beneath the dome a great crown of light descends upon the main altar.

There is a papal throne at the end of the apsis, another in the Gregorian chapel, another in the portico, another on the balcony facing St. Peter's Square.

The façade of the Basilica and the outside of the dome are

lined with thousands of electric lights. At coronations before the discovery of electricity tens of thousands of candles and torches were installed on the outside of the church, and it speaks well for the skill of the Sanpietrini that church annals record no fires.

The Sanpietrini set up fences on the Piazza for there and on nearby streets and rooftops fully a million people will assemble. Perhaps six hundred thousand will actually see the Pope. The others will see some part of the great event—foreign dignitaries, pilgrims in national costume, the Cardinals—and will hear the Pope's voice broadcast by loudspeakers.

Though St. Peter's Square belongs to the Vatican, since it is an integral part of Rome, it is not separated from the rest of the city by walls. During the Coronation its status is symbolically indicated by fences before which Italian troops are stationed. This outer entrance to the Vatican State is guarded by papal gendarmes. About twenty yards before the entrance to the Basilica is a line of fences which can be passed only by those who are invited inside the church. Along this line are detachments of the papal Palatine Guard.

The Palatine Guard was formed in 1850 during the pontificate of Pius IX. Its five hundred members are recruited from Italian families and are charged with general guard service during ceremonies. They wear red shakos and trousers and blue jackets with epaulettes.

Once papal guards fought battles. Now their significance is limited. During the Nazi occupation of Rome, however, the Palatine Guard was reenforced and numbered about two thousand. They are not warriors but if necessary they would die in defense of the Pope.

All the entrances of the Vatican and St. Peter's Church are manned by Swiss Guards whose first two hundred members arrived in Rome in 1506, hired by Pope Julius II because the Swiss were known as courageous soldiers.

Today the Swiss Guard consists of the Commander, five officers, six sergeants, ninety corporals and guards. In their own nomenclature, they call the sergeants officers too, because the nomenclature remain the same as their uniform of the sixteenth century.

Their commander is a prominent member of the papal court. At the Coronation they are dressed in half-medieval, half-Renaissance uniforms partly designed by Michelangelo. Breast and back are covered with armor and they wear a high medieval helmet. Their dress consists of tunic, breeches, stockings with wide yellow, blue and red stripes, white ruff and steel morion to which a steel breastplate is added. They are armed with halberds and swords.

First among the guards of the Pontiff are the members of the papal Noble Guard. Founded by Pius VII in 1801, it consists of two hundred men, all members of the Italian nobility, who accompany the Pope from the moment of his election until his coffin is walled in.

The nomenclature of the Noble Guard is Napoleonic; i.e., it stems from the late eighteenth and early nineteenth century. Their General Staff consists of four Lieutenant Generals (always in the Napoleonic sense). One of these Lieutenant Generals is the Commander of the Guard. Another Lieutenant General—not the Commander—carries the title of Standardbearer of the Holy Roman Church. This title with the Lieutenant General rank in the guard is hereditary in the family of the Marquess Patrizi Montoro of Rome.

At the Coronation ceremonies, the Noble Guard's uniform is bearskin headgear, or helmet white breeches, blue tunic with crossed belts, top boots and saber.

On the day the Coronation takes place, the flow of spectators to St. Peter's Square begins around four o'clock in the morning. By eight o'clock the Square and the streets leading to it are a human sea in continuous motion. There are pilgrims from all over the world; Italian police records show that nearly every race and nation are represented. Most of the people, however, are Romans, an extraordinary fact when one recalls that the total population of Rome is only about two million. During a Coronation the citizens of the city, even adversaries of the Church, seem to feel a mystical sense of unity with the Bishop of Rome.

Those who, though they have received official invitations, have no assigned seats in the Basilica, try to get in soon after the doors open at six o'clock. Men have black suits on; women wear long black dresses with black veils covering the head. Civilians with specially assigned seats wear tailcoats with black vest and white tie. Diplomats wear their tailed diplomatic uniforms. Military men arrive in their brilliant dress uniforms, priests and members of religious orders in their usual garb. All are aware of the fact that they are participating in the greatest ceremony in the modern world.

While the people in the Basilica and St. Peter's Square prepare to make the Coronation a truly Roman festival, the Pope is vested in the sacred garments he will wear in the procession that, starting from the papal apartments, will reach the main altar of St. Peter's Church. Meanwhile the procession is forming. Everyone in it knows his place for written instructions have been sent to all. Fully a hundred persons, led by the Chief Master of Ceremonies, are assigned to the task of directing the procession and other activities. They accompany the Pope, Cardinals and everyone else who has even the smallest function during the papal Mass and the act of Coronation and they give the signs that ensure the even flow of the day's dramatic events.

The day of the Coronation is always a Sunday or Holy Day. In the morning, when all the Cardinals are gathered in the Vatican's Sala Paramenti, the Pope, in his white cassock with a purple ermine-lined mantle around his shoulders, descends from his apartment accompanied by two Noble Guards flanked by two officers of the Swiss Guard, followed by his personal physician and his valet in tailcoats and surrounded by Chamberlains, two of them wearing black court dress with white ruff around the neck. Slowly they proceed through the ten large rooms between the papal apartment and the Sala Clementina.

At the door of the Sala Clementina, named after Pope Clement VIII (1592–1605) who rebuilt it, a Swiss Guard stands at attention. Against a wall of the room stand ten others, as honor guard. There is no furniture in the room but it does not look bare because of its large paintings, one of them representing St. Clement's martyrdom.

Here occurs the first ceremony of the day: the vesting of the Pope.

3. *The Pageantry of the Procession*

It would take volumes to describe in detail the origins and traditions of the garments the Pope will wear today. Their importance lies in the fact that the Pontiff is about to perform a divine service. In the Catholic Church the Holy Mass is an offer of sacrifice to God, a mystical occurrence because, according to Catholic belief, in every Mass God Himself is offered as a sacrifice repeating the sacrifice on the Cross. It is therefore proper that all who participate in this mystery be reverently attired.

Of these papal garments the alb, which is of Roman and Greek origin, is made of white linen and reaches from neck to ankles. It symbolizes purity of heart. The stole, again a remnant of old Rome, is a symbol of immortality of which man is unworthy. The large white mantle, the *manto,* is a sign of authority and for thousands of years has been worn by Jews, Persians and Chinese with that significance. The pectoral cross, hanging on a chain around the neck, is a sign of episcopal authority; it contains the relic of a saint. The mitre, adorned with gold and precious stones, which a Cardinal places upon the Pope's head, symbolizes the helmet of salvation. The Pope will remove it whenever he prays.

The *sedia gestatoria,* the portable throne, Oriental in origin, was first used in the western world by Charlemagne and later by other emperors. The two ceremonial fans made of ostrich plumes on long staffs, called flabelli, originated in Egypt; at one time they were made of peacock feathers and the eye-shaped designs were said to symbolize the constant vigilance of the Pope over the whole world. The canopy, or baldachino, held by four prelates, had its origin in Bagdad.

In the large rooms in which the papal cortege forms, the Cardinals in long scarlet robes are grouped not according to national origin but according to rank and function. Each Cardinal is accompanied by his secretary and his *caudatario,* a priest who holds the train of the Cardinal's mantle.

The train of a Cardinal's mantle was nine feet long until recently. Pope Pius XII, in his order of November 30, 1952, shortened the train which now is prescribed to be four and a half feet.

Laymen dressed in the tight-fitting black court uniforms of the Renaissance are the Cardinals' *gentiluomini,* or chamberlains.

The three hundred or more Patriarchs, Archbishops and Bishops are in two groups: those who are assistants to the papal throne and who therefore in this procession and in other ceremonies stand comparatively close to His Holiness; and those who are not. The two groups are the most colorful in the procession.

Those who belong to the Latin Rite, or in other words to the western world, can be distinguished by their dress from those who belong to one of the Oriental Rites. Archbishops, Bishops and the higher ranking Abbots of the western world all wear mitres, of varying shapes, but do not carry the curved Bishop's staff.

No Archbishop, Patriarch, or Abbot is allowed to carry Episcopal Staff in the presence of the Pope. Bishops residing in Rome may use it only at benedictions at afternoon vespers, or when a new Bishop is consecrated. Only the

Bishop of Rome, the Pope, has the right to the Episcopal Staff. His staff is a long one ending in a triple cross.

Those who possess ancient robes which have outlasted the vicissitudes of time are allowed to wear them. Many Bishops of the western world wear the habits of the religious orders to which they belong.

Patriarchs and Bishops of the Eastern Rites wear crowns instead of mitres. Their Episcopal Staffs end in a cross, sometimes a triple cross.

Bishops of the Slavonic Rites are readily differentiated because of their robes.

In the procession, in which about two thousand individuals participate, are bearded Arabs from Syria, Lebanon and other Near Eastern countries. Their communities, dating back to the first centuries after Christ, have preserved a good deal of independence in administration and liturgy and this is reflected in their dress. Bishops of the Coptic (Abyssinian) and Malabar (Indian) Rites wear the heaviest vestments, so richly embroidered with gold that from a distance they look like gold plate.

In the groups of Patriarchs, Archbishops and Bishops, the endless variations in appearance suggest the true universality of the Church.

The Cardinals and the Bishops, with the Patriarchs and Archbishops, form the most important group around the new Pope. They are the core of the Church. There is a saying from St. Cyprian which expresses the Bishop's unique position in the Catholic Church; according to St. Cyprian the Church is in the Bishop and the Bishop is within the Church; consequently, anyone who is not with the Bishop is not with the Church. That is why such prominence is given to Bishops at the Coronation of a Pope. Other court functionaries may wear more colorful uniforms; none can surpass the Bishops in authority, dignity and importance.

A papal procession is, of course, composed according to established rules inherent in the hierarchical structure of the Church and in any court procedure, but it is also affected by changing customs. The Pope is a sovereign, recognized as such by the whole world, and all sovereigns live with a certain formality, according to protocol. The papal court is the oldest in the world and has preserved a wealth of traditions from East and West. Yet the outward forms of the procession and of the other ceremonies are recognized as comparatively unimportant. Nothing is essential save the spirit by which the ceremonies are animated.

It is said that in the sixteenth century King Francis I of France, having witnessed a papal procession, later remarked to Pope Leo X maliciously: "Your Holiness, the first followers of Christ wore simply sheepskin."

The Pope had a ready answer: "Those were times, Your Majesty, when kings herded the sheep," meaning that the ways of one age cannot be judged from the perspective of another.

It is self-evident to Pope, Bishops, mendicant monks and laymen, to all who participate in this Coronation, that gold, velvet, jewels and historical pageantry would have no value, on the contrary might even work harm, if they were not the outcome of purity of heart and desire to please God by external symbols of respect. All know that mere processions and ceremonies will not lead the wicked to Heaven.

When the Pope is vested and everyone is in his place, the papal crossbearer, a high prelate in a long purple cape, genuflects before the Pontiff and waits for a word from the Chief of the Masters of Ceremonies. It is the Latin word *Extra* (Out), uttered in a firm loud voice. Since the large halls of the Vatican in which the procession forms are connected by open doors, the *Extra* rolls above the heads of the participants down to those who are in the lead. Slowly the procession gets under way.

Its first stop will be in the portico of St. Peter's Basilica, which can easily hold two thousand persons. It is empty now, but the papal throne close to the main entrance is ready.

In the church and on the Square the multitude grows agitated. Loudspeakers have conveyed the word *Extra* to the people and they are listening to a description of the procession, seeing in imagination how this river of ecclesiastical and historical costume moves forward.

First come the mendicant orders. Then the monastics and after them the canons regular. The procession is not only arranged according to rank but, within the ranks, according to seniority. On both sides of the cortege, there are more and more accompanying papal ushers, couriers, guards and lay dignitaries. The closer one marches to the Pope, the higher one's rank is. The mendicant, monastic orders and the canons regular consider themselves the most humble. This is why they open the procession. The mendicants, like the Dominicans, lived from day to day from alms. So did the friars minor Conventual and the Capuchins who, with the Augustinians, Mercedarians, and the Minims comprise the little group of mendicants, some in brown cassocks with white cord around the waist, others in black or, as the Dominicans, in white. There are great preachers, professors and scientists among this group, as well as among the next one, which is the group of the monastic orders, comprising the different Benedictine categories, the Cistercians and the Camaldolite monks. Centuries of history pass before the eyes of the people. Among the Cistercians, we see the Trappists in white robes like the Carthusians, their hair shaved off the top of the skull. The canons regular comprise the Premonstratensians; then the canons regular of St. Augustin with several congregations, among them the canons regular of the Lateran of our Holy Redeemer and the canons regular of the Most Holy Cross.

No members of any other religious order take part in any papal procession, only those listed above. The papal procession includes members of religious orders founded before 1474.* This has a historical explanation. It was St. Ignatius who asked Pope Paul III (1534–1549) not to include the members of the Jesuit Order in any papal procession because the many Roman ceremonies would take too much time. The Pope consented and ever since it became habit that only the canons regular, the mendicant and the monastic orders take part in papal processions.

The members of the religious orders are followed by the large representation of the Roman clergy. Black cassocked Roman priests in white alb, then the dignitaries of the Collegiate and Basilica Churches of Rome with their respective clergy. It is their privilege to carry in the procession the Cross and the *ombrellone* of their respective Basilica. The

* The Minims appeared that year.

Lateran Basilica, the Church of the Bishop of Rome (the Pope), is the highest ranking church of the Catholic world, and thus has two crosses. No standards or flags are carried by religious or the priests in the Coronation procession. These are carried only in a canonization cortege.

Members of the religious orders, the Roman clergy, and the clergy of the Basilicas in the procession amount to five hundred people.

This group is divided from the next one by two sergeants of the Swiss guard who do not bear halberds, but canes with a little ribbon. With the two Swiss begins the real papal court. The papal crossbearer follows; the Cross is carried by an auditor (*uditore*) of the Secret Rota, a high-ranking prelate in purple. This section of the procession is far the largest and the costumes vary.

Lay chamberlains of honor, chamberlains of *Spada e Cappa* (with a cape and sword) follow. Their office existed since 1555. They are vested in their so-called *Spagnola*, i.e., Spanish dress which consists of a black tunic almost down to their knees, a mantle of black velvet, black silk stockings, and a huge white collar around the neck. After these laymen more priests follow: the Apostolic Preacher, a Capuchin, who usually becomes a Bishop after he is released from his duties; the Confessor of the Papal Household, who is always a Servite (the Order of the Servants of Mary); then the Common Chaplains, the Honorary Privy Chaplains, the Consistorial Advocates (some of them laymen), the Honorary and Supernumerary Privy Chamberlains, and the Privy Chamberlain's Participant. In their dioceses in Germany, Spain, Canada or wherever, these men, who for the most part are church administrators, are highly honored, but their titles become living realities only in Rome during papal functions.

The next part of the cortege is mostly composed by judges and their aides of the two highest ecclesiastical tribunals, the Rota, and the Apostolic Signatura, the latter being the Highest Court of Appeal. The Master of the Sacred Palaces walks alone. He is always a Dominican and it is his task to take care of the Index, the list of prohibited books. As long as the Papal States existed, he was the official censor.

One prelate, surrounded by Bussolanti (lay chamberlain ushers serving in the Vatican Palace) carries on a cushion the tiara. Two Privy Chaplains carry in their hands the two mitres the Pope is going to use during the solemn papal Mass. The Grand Master of the Sacred Hospice, a title which was not given to anyone after the recent death of the Prince Ruspoli, is the first of the four papal lay chamberlains who are the highest ranking laymen in the papal court. This office goes back to the sixth century. His task nowadays is mostly confined to great receptions, particularly to such audiences, when a sovereign is received by the Pope.

This group comprises those prelates who carry the sacred vestments of the Pope for the Mass. Then three prelates carry the incense or thurible, suspended on a long golden chain. Then seven dignitaries carry seven candlesticks with ornamented candles. Follows the Apostolic Subdeacon who is an auditor of the Rota and who will assist at the Mass together with one of the Cardinal Deacons. Next are the Penitentiaries of St. Peter's, some of whom have heard confessions in the Basilica for three or four decades. They wear over their black habit the chasuble and carry their long wooden staff, now decorated with laurel. According to an old custom, at certain times penitents may, if they wish, kneel before the penitentiary and receive a light tap on the head with the staff, and by this public act acknowledge themselves to be sinners. The custom seems to date back to the ninth century.

In the group that follows there are Abbots, heads of monasteries, simple monks like their brethren at the head of the procession. These, however, have the privilege of wearing the mitre at certain occasions, such as the great one today.

The Monsignor Commendatore of the Santo Spirito, is next, a high-ranking prelate, head of all priests assigned to religious assistance in the hospitals of Rome. His name derives from the first hospital created in Rome, the Hospital of the Holy Ghost (Santo Spirito), which was built by Gregory the Great for pilgrims from the British Isles.

And now the cortege assumes even greater solemnity. Appearing are the Bishops, Archbishops and Patriarchs, first those who have the title Assistants at the Papal Throne, then the others.

Each priest carries great responsibility because, according to Catholic belief, he can absolve and bind. The Bishops, of course, possessing "the fullness of priesthood," have even greater responsibility and in addition must know how to handle the problems of the world, for they are in constant contact with secular authorities. Here in this magnificent procession, the Bishops receive equal consideration. They walk a little apart from one another, the distance between them suggesting their different individual jurisdictions. Their mantles float extended like so many royal robes and indeed

some of them, with mitres and crowns upon their heads, resemble princes. Only the Cardinals, however, are called
Princes of the Church.

Of the Sacred College of Cardinals, one keen American
observer had much to say, and every word is valid. Wrote
Francis A. MacNutt, in his book *A Papal Chamberlain*
(Longmans, Green, New York, 1936): "Who and what are
they? First of all, the great number of them are old men who
have reached the highest dignity to which they can aspire
and of which nobody and nothing can deprive them. . . .
Each of them has received the Cardinalate for sufficient reasons: either for his exceptional learning, his eminent piety,
because of the importance of the Episcopal See he governs
or as a natural reward for services in pontifical diplomacy."

In the Coronation procession they walk unspeaking, smiling or serious according to their natures, each with the train
of his scarlet mantle carried by a *caudatario.*

Now the first macebearers arrive—the mace is a symbol of
sovereignty—laymen in medieval dress wearing tight-fitting
trunks, blue berets and open jackets. Raphael the painter
once was such a macebearer. Succeeding the bearers are other
court attendants, laymen carrying the *virga rubea,* a purple
stick; in Renaissance times at certain ceremonies they directed the flow of crowds. And now the first tall Noble
Guards are discernible, which means that the Pope is near.

In purple *cappa,* alone, walks a high-ranking prelate, the
Vice-Camerlengo of the Holy Roman Church. Then come
two laymen in fifteenth century court dress, with large ruf-
fled collars around their necks. One is the head of the Colonna family, the other the oldest Orsini; they are princes

whose ancestry goes back almost to Roman times. Both are assistants to the papal throne; they perform certain services during solemn functions of the Pope.

Two Cardinals, separated from their fellows, succeed them. They will assist the Pope in celebrating Mass.

The papal Master of Ceremonies with two assistants appears now and, following him, an officer in dark blue uniform, a round busbee with a plume on his head and bronze sword in hand. He is the Commander of the Palatine Guard. Strikingly uniformed too is the Colonel (Commander) of the Swiss Guard, who wears white, yellow and blue striped tunic, breeches and stockings. The Commander of the papal Noble Guard wears high black boots with spurs, white breeches and a black busbee.

There is another Roman prince, the Postmaster-General of the Vatican, a title and office hereditary in the Massimo family, and then the Deputy Master of Ceremonies. Now all realize that at last the Pope is close.

The portable throne is surrounded by at least fifty persons. Twelve *sediari*, thronebearers, six on each side, carry it. They wear white gloves, white silk, stiff-collared shirts, crimson damask breeches and a coat of damask reaching to the knee.

On the left of the throne is the standardbearer of the Holy Roman Church, who wears cuirassier's helmet with plume, blue tunic with crossed black belts, white breeches and black topboots. Ten other officers of the Noble Guard are also around the throne, and there are three laymen in fifteenth century gold-embroidered black court dress, with golden

chains and keys around their necks. They are highest ranking chamberlains.

At each corner of the *sedia gestatoria* walks a Swiss Guards-
man holding a sword slanting forward. The canopy above
the papal throne is the largest and most elaborate in the
world. It is fastened to four poles, held by four prelates,
members of the high ecclesiastical tribunal, the Rota. The
two ceremonial fans are carried behind the throne by two
private chamberlains in gold-embroidered scarlet tunics with
velvet lapels.

The Pope, in a long gold cape called a *falda* worn only by
pontiffs, rests his left hand on an arm of the throne and with
his right continually imparts his Benediction. On his head is
the precious mitre.

This is the Pope's first official function and his first public
appearance in the *sedia gestatoria*. All eyes are upon him.
When the throne approaches, people kneel in reverence before the successor of St. Peter. (The papal Benediction, like
any other Benediction coming from God's Grace, must be
received on both knees.)

Behind the throne are more prelates, in purple capes and
ermine collars, then the chiefs of those religious orders whose
members marched at the head of the procession. Bussolanti
and couriers close the walking after the Pope's private valet
and his personal physician.

And now the Pope has arrived at the entrance of the portico of St. Peter's Basilica and the central Coronation ceremony begins.

4. *The Papal Mass*

In a corner of the immense portico, the choir of the Basilica (the Capella Giulia, founded by Julius III [1550–1555]) launches into the ancient hymn beginning with the words *Tu es Petrus*. This is the first greeting the new Pontiff receives. Descending from the *sedia,* he mounts the throne already prepared in the portico and listens to a few words in Latin addressed to him by the Basilica's Cardinal Archpriest. The Cardinal kisses the Pontiff's ring and, genuflecting, kisses the embroidered Cross on the Pope's right shoe. (The liturgical kiss signifies honor and reverence.)

Then the members of the clergy of St. Peter's Church—about 55—step before the Pope and kiss his feet while the choir sings the verses of the *Tu es Petrus* hymn. The hymn ceases only when the Pope again has mounted the *sedia gestatoria* and the procession slowly enters the front door of St. Peter's Church. Then there is almost absolute silence.

It is rarely dim in this gigantic church because of the sunlight which enters through its great windows but now, with hundreds of thousands of lights ablaze, the scene is truly radiant.

The silence is shattered by the sound of twelve trumpets. Members of the band of the Palatine Guard play the Marcia Triomfale of Silveri. At the beginning they are heard clearly but soon other sounds drown them out—the sounds of the vast congregation greeting the new Pope.

Each of the scores of thousands of people in the church waves something: little flags with the yellow and white papal colors; flags of their own countries; branches of olive trees; handkerchiefs. It is a spontaneous demonstration of love.

Ceaselessly the Pope imparts his Benediction and smiling turns to right and left.

The ovation stops as suddenly as if someone had given a sign. The *sedia gestatoria* is carried to the Chapel of the Holy Sacrament on the right side of the Basilica, close to the altar where stands the world-famous *Pietà* of Michelangelo. Before the portable throne is lowered to the floor, the Pope removes his mitre to pray.

He prays for perhaps ten minutes in the Chapel of the Holy Sacrament before the Holy Eucharist is placed in a monstrance on the altar. On this day when he is so fervently praised and receives obedience, the Pope, the absolute spiritual sovereign of the Catholic Church, expresses his own absolute obedience to God.

Except for the actual crowning of the Pope, the Coronation ceremony in the Basilica is part of the Pontifical Mass. For the Mass all priests are attired in sacred vestments of symbolical meaning. The vesting of the Pope is performed in another chapel, also on the right side of St. Peter's Church, called the Chapel of St. Gregory. A part of the procession therefore moves to this chapel. Another part takes its place near the Basilica's main altar. In the Chapel of St. Gregory the Pope prays again, this time kneeling on the *Faldistero*, a *prie-dieu* which only he may use.

At this point, the entire Sacred College of Cardinals again expresses obedience to the Pontiff. The venerable princes of the Church kneel before him and kiss his right hand. Then, while the crossbearer stands at his right side, he blesses the

Cardinals with the words *"Sit nomen Domini benedictum."* ("Blessed be the name of God.")

The help of the Holy Ghost is invoked before the vesting begins. The so-called Divine Office, a sequence of meditations said in prayer each day by every priest and all members of religious communities, is divided according to the day's periods. This is the terce, or in Latin *tertia,* which commemorates the descent of the Holy Ghost on the Apostles. One of the Cardinals intones the first prayer and the choir responds. The angelic Gregorian chant fills the air and the choir continues to sing while the Pope and the Cardinals are attired in the robes of their office.

The Pope's large mantle is replaced by the dalmatic, the Mass vestment of a Deacon, and over it the chasuble, the Mass vestment of an ordained priest which resembles a yoke and signifies that he is in the yoke of God. The Pontiff receives the stole and his mitre is put back upon his head. All these vestments, weighing some sixty pounds, are elaborately fastened with belts to distribute the weight.

When the Pontiff is ready, two Cardinals from the order of the Cardinal Deacons step to his side and will not leave his throne until the end of the Coronation. Another Cardinal Deacon and a Cardinal Bishop will assist him at the altar.

As one of the Cardinal Deacons lifts his staff, the ferule, the Pope in a voice that reaches all corners of the Basilica gives his permission for the celebrants of the Mass to proceed to the altar: *"Procedamus in pace."* ("Let us proceed in peace.") The choir responds with joy: *"In nomine Christ. . . ."* (In Christ's name. . . .")

The Pope is lifted by the *sediari* and the procession to the main altar begins. Another ovation breaks out but abruptly ends. The Church provides for a wise balance in each ceremony. Thus the Pope on this day of glory is reminded by means of a burner and a handful of flax that the human being is as nothing before God and that the material world will crumble and vanish whenever He so desires. The Pope himself three times puts the flax into the little burner held by the Master of Ceremonies. And three times as the flax flames and the smoke disappears the Master of Ceremonies reminds him: *"Sic transit gloria mundi."* ("Thus passes the glory of the world.")

As the *sedia gestatoria* is carried to the main altar, it passes before the ancient seated statue of St. Peter, the first Pope. Pope St. Leo I, after he had met Attila and forced a withdrawal of the Scourge of God from the gates of Rome, erected it in grateful recognition of the salvation of the City. The statue of St. Peter soon became the most revered of all statues for the people of Rome. On June 29, the feast day of St. Peter, it is dressed in papal vestments and has been for more than a thousand years.

The *sedia gestatoria* is placed in front of the papal altar toward the apse. There could hardly be a more appropriate setting for a solemn papal Mass than this main altar under the dome of the world's greatest church.

Around the altar the floor is clear in a radius of about twenty yards. Members of the procession are around this almost circular space, the Cardinals seated on their benches in the apse. The papal throne is at the end of the apse. The whole apse is covered with red carpet, its design showing the tiara and the keys of papal authority. Members of the Noble

Guard, Swiss Guard and Palatine Guard stand with drawn swords. Around the steps of the altar are small tables with sacred objects for the Mass: chalice, cruets, candles, white linen clothes called purifiers, a golden spoon, a golden tube, an incense boat, the Book of the Gospels, and the Book of the Epistles.

The papal Mass does not differ essentially from any other Mass celebrated in a Catholic church. The Low Mass is its simplest form. The High Mass is a Mass in which certain parts are sung by the celebrating priest in a Gregorian chant and the choir responds. A Solemn Mass is one in which the celebrating priest is assisted by other priests and by deacons, acolytes and others. The celebrating priest is the one who consecrates the Host and the wine; it is the act which transubstantiates them into Christ's body and blood. This, the repetition of Christ's sacrifice on the Cross, is the heart of any Mass.

The papal Mass is a Solemn Mass in which the celebrant is assisted by Cardinals, Bishops and others who perform the functions of deacons, acolytes, and so on. Basically it is the Mass of an Archbishop; it also has elements, some of them dating back to the third century, peculiar to the Mass of the Pope and reveals the historical continuity within the Church. The beginnings of the liturgy go back to the year 96, to the time of St. Clement.

According to their function, the assisting Cardinals and prelates stand on the steps of the altar and around the papal throne. The little tables, called Sacristy tables, are surrounded by assistants wearing the white alb. At the throne stand two Cardinals, two Swiss Guards with double-edged swords, the

Commanders of the Papal Guards and the Chief of the Masters of Ceremonies.

Only the Guardsmen continue to stand still. The Mass is action; in the Catholic belief, it is the highest human and divine drama. The assisting Cardinals, Bishops, prelates and others are seldom motionless, and each move they make has symbolic significance.

Since the essence of the Mass is the sacrifice, the most ancient form of worship, the first parts of the Mass are a preparation. After the sacrifice and the Communion come expressions of gratitude for graces received. Although the Mass is much the same as if it were celebrated by a simple priest, it is one of the great moments in Christian affairs when the Pope, bareheaded, stands at the altar at the beginning of the Mass and publicly, with deep bow, confesses his sins and asks for forgiveness.

All but two parts of the Mass, the reading of the Epistle and of the Gospel, are celebrated in Latin, because Rome belongs to the Latin Rite of the Catholic Church. The *Confiteor* is said in Latin, and it is repeated by all the Cardinals and prelates and participating clergy.

Up to this point there has been no change in the ordinary flow of the Mass, but now it is interrupted for the first major act connected with the Coronation proper, the placing of the pallium around the Pope's neck and shoulders.

The pallium, a circular band of white wool two inches wide, is decorated with six crosses and has a pendant strip before and behind. Only the Pope may wear it at all times. It is granted to Archbishops and Bishops to symbolize the fullness of Episcopal power. In ancient times it indicated that the Bishop who received it from the Pope had gained special merit by his obedience to the Holy See. The pallium is made of the wool of two lambs. It is blessed in the Church of St. Agnes in Rome on her feast day, blessed again by the Pope on the feast day of St. Peter and then stored in a casket near the tomb of St. Peter.

The pallium is placed upon the shoulders of the Pope by a Cardinal who receives it from a genuflecting prelate. Holding the sacred object in his extended hands, the Cardinal solemnly recites in Latin the formula: "Receive the sacred pallium which signifies the fullness of thy pontifical office for the honor of the omnipotent God and the Most Glorious Virgin Mary, His Mother, and for the honor of the Blessed Apostles, Peter and Paul, and for the honor of the Holy Roman Church."

Bowing, bareheaded, the Pope steps up to the altar and performs the ceremony of incensing, whereupon the assisting Cardinals kiss his left cheek and his pectoral cross. Then follows an additional demonstration of obedience in which all the Cardinals, Bishops, Patriarchs, Abbots, prelates and the Penitentiaries of St. Peter participate. The Cardinals, bareheaded, kiss the Pontiff's feet and right hand and the Pope embraces them. The Patriarchs, Archbishops and Bishops kiss his feet and right knee. The Abbots and the Penitentiaries kiss his feet. The Mass then proceeds.

It is interrupted again by an occurrence proper to all coronations and not merely to the Coronation of the Pope—the praising of the person to be crowned.

The so-called "Praise" of the Pope actually is more an invocation to God and the saints to help him. Parts of the papal cortege, including the assisting Cardinals, guards and macebearers, walk around the main altar to the entrance of St. Peter's Tomb. The officiating Cardinals' invocation begins the ceremony. The participants are divided into two groups responding to each other.

"Hearken, O God, to our prayers for our master, Pope. . . ."

"Saviour of the world."

"Help him, help him."

"St. Michael and St. Gabriel."

"Help him, help him."

The next part of the Mass is peculiar to solemn papal Masses: the Epistle and the Gospel are sung in both Latin and Greek, expressing the unity of East and West in the Catholic Church.

The event is divided into small, detailed ceremonies. The Book of the Epistles and the Book of the Gospels are incensed. Those who sing say a special prayer, begging God to cleanse their mouths while they pronounce the eternal words. The acolytes bring candles, not for light but to express the joy that accompanies listening to the words of the Lord. The Pope blesses the Books and those who bring them to him kiss his feet. All these acts have a single meaning: to honor the Word.

Nearing the center of the Mass—the consecration of the Host and the wine—the liturgical movements become more elaborate. The significance is obvious. The paten upon which the Host will be placed and later consecrated, the chalice which will hold the wine that transubstantiates into the Precious Blood, are blessed and cleaned. The hands of all, including those of the Pope himself, are blessed and purified in a series of comings and goings from the Sacristy tables. In addition, those responsible for the Host and the wine must prove that both are pure.

This act is now entirely symbolic, but it recalls doleful years of the tenth century when vicious men killed priests and popes by poisoning the wine and the Host. The prelates who bring them to the Pope taste them first.

Unforgettable is the scene in which the Pope pronounces the words *"Sanctus, sanctus, sanctus Dominus Deus."* ("Holy, holy, holy is our Lord.")

The seventy-five or eighty thousand people in the Basilica kneel in silence. The Guardsmen lower their swords. Eight prelates, accompanied by a Master of Ceremonies, hold lighted torches before the altar. And when the Pope elevates the Sacred Host after having consecrated it, trumpets in the dome of the Basilica play a sacred melody, the *Largo* of Longhi, who was a member of the Noble Guard in the eighteenth century. Pope Leo XIII forbade the playing of the *Largo* of Longhi at any other ceremony than that of the elevation during the papal Mass.

Bells are not used at Masses celebrated by the Pope or in the presence of the Pope. The ringing of bells was introduced toward the end of the Middle Ages but the popes never allowed this innovation in their chapels.

Three times the Pope elevates the Host and the chalice, before him and then to the right and to the left. Any other priest would elevate it only before him.

The most moving part of the papal Mass is the ceremony before the Communion. Communion means the union with Christ in the spirit of peace and love of all men. Before the

Pope takes Communion—that is, before consuming the Host and the Precious Blood—standing before the altar he embraces the Cardinals who have assisted him. This is the Kiss of Peace. The embrace will be repeated several hundred times. One Cardinal after another receives it, then the lowest ranking Cardinal embraces the first Patriarch and the lowest ranking Patriarch embraces the first Archbishop, and so on down to the participating prelates.

As every priest does, the Pope takes Communion "under two signs," which means that he consumes both the Host and the Precious Blood (laymen receive only the Host). It is a privilege of the Pope to take the Precious Blood from the chalice through a golden tube. Before receiving the Celestial Bread he strikes his breast like any other sinner, saying: "*Domine, non sum dignus. . . .*" ("I am not worthy, O Lord. . . .") Each drop of the Precious Blood and each particle of the Host must be consumed.

Now the assisting Cardinals and the Sacristan purify the paten, cleanse the chalice and consume the water mixed with the Precious Blood.

5. *The Act of Coronation*

The papal Mass ends. One of the Cardinals replaces the gloves, the skullcap and the Episcopal ring on the Pope's hands; they had been removed before he touched the chalice and the Host. The Pope mounts the *sedia gestatoria* and the mitre is placed upon his head as the multitude bursts into exclamations of good wishes and joy.

The papal procession winds its way through the congregation and stops at the Chapel of the Holy Sacrament, where the Pope prays. Then it leaves through the great bronze doors of the Basilica, passing through the portico and mounting the Sala Regia that leads to the huge balcony of St. Peter's facing the Square. The balcony on which the Coronation ceremony will be performed is adorned with a large canopy, under which a throne awaits the Pope. A thirty-foot carpet, decorated with the Pontiff's coat of arms, is lowered over the balcony railing.

For the multitude on St. Peter's Square which has not seen the papal Mass and has participated in it only by listening to the prayers and the description broadcast through loudspeakers, this will be the climax. For the Pope it will be the final symbol of the burdens that were put upon him by his election as Vicar of Christ and Supreme Shepherd of hundreds of millions of Christians.

After the tiara is on his head, the ceremonies end abruptly. There will be no banquets with toasts, felicitations and festivities. The hard, tenacious life that is ahead of him begins. As his predecessors did, he will return from the balcony of the Basilica to his austere apartment, to solitude.

When he appears on the balcony the people gathered before him do not think of this. They cheer endlessly, stopping only when the choir intones the ancient hymn *Corona Aurea Super Caput Eius* (A Golden Crown is Placed Upon His Head). This should be a joyful chant, but today it sounds solemnly severe.

After the hymn the Dean of the Sacred College of Cardinals recites the Lord's Prayer, the simplest and at the same time the most magnificent prayer of all. It is the only prayer that accompanies the act of Coronation. There are no oaths, no special liturgical ceremonies. The Pope is seated on the throne. One of the Cardinals removes the mitre from his head and the Dean of the Sacred College summons the prelate holding the tiara. Then he approaches the Pope, kneels and, with the tiara in his hands, pronounces the formula: "Accept this ornate tiara of the three crowns and remember that you are Father of the Princes and Kings, Pontiff of the world and Vicar of Our Saviour Jesus Christ on this earth, whose honor and glory will last through centuries and centuries."

Now the Cardinal rises and places the tiara upon the Pontiff's head.

The Pope is crowned. He imparts his first threefold Benediction in the name of the Father and the Son and the Holy Ghost, looking at the crowd, a million individuals with a million private lives and a million souls, looking too into the distance beyond the mountains of Rome. When he gives the Apostolic Blessing he smiles and the multitude cheers, because he and they know that our only hope lies in the infinite pity of God in Whose name he conveys the Benediction.

Appendix

I

THE POPES
A List of the Supreme Pontiffs

Name	Birthplace	Accession	End of Reign
St. Peter	Judea		64 or 67
St. Linus	Tuscia	67	76
St. Anacletus (Cletus)	Rome	76	88
St. Clement	Rome	88	97
St. Evaristus	Greece	97	105
St. Alexander I	Rome	105	115
St. Sixtus I	Rome	115	125
St. Telesphorus	Greece	125	136
St. Hyginus	Greece	136	140
St. Pius I	Aquileia	140	155
St. Anicetus	Syria	155	166
St. Soterus	Campania	166	175
St. Eleutherius	Nicopoli in Epirus	175	189
St. Victor I	Africa	189	199
St. Zephyrinus	Rome	199	217
St. Callistus I	Rome	217	222
St. Urban I	Rome	222	230
St. Pontian	Rome	July 21, 230	Sept. 28, 235
St. Anterus	Greece	Nov. 21, 235	Jan. 3, 236
St. Fabian	Rome	Jan. 10, 236	Jan. 20, 250
St. Cornelius	Rome	Mar., 251	June, 253
St. Lucius I	Rome	June 25, 253	Mar. 5, 254
St. Stephen I	Rome	May 12, 254	Aug. 2, 257
St. Sixtus II	Greece	Aug. 30, 257	Aug. 6, 258
St. Dionysius	unknown	July 22, 259	Dec. 26, 268
St. Felix I	Rome	Jan. 5, 269	Dec. 30, 274
St. Eutychian	Luni	Jan. 4, 275	Dec. 7, 283
St. Caius	Dalmatia	Dec. 17, 283	Apr. 22, 296

THE POPES

Name	*Birthplace*	*Accession*	*End of Reign*
St. Marcellinus	Rome	June 30, 296	Oct. 25, 304
St. Marcellus I	Rome	May 27, 308 or June 26, 308	Jan. 16, 309
St. Eusebius	Greece	Apr. 18, 309 or 310	Aug. 17, 309 or 310
St. Melchiades	Africa	July 2, 311	Jan. 11, 314
St. Sylvester I	Rome	Jan. 31, 314	Dec. 31, 335
St. Marcus	Rome	Jan. 18, 336	Oct. 7, 336
St. Julius I	Rome	Feb. 6, 337	Apr. 12, 352
Liberius	Rome	May 17, 352	Sept. 24, 366
St. Damasus I	Spain	Oct. 1, 366	Dec. 11, 384
St. Siricius	Rome	Dec. 15 or 22 or 29, 384.	Nov. 26, 399
St. Anastasius I	Rome	Nov. 27, 399	Dec. 19, 401
St. Innocent I	Albano	Dec. 22, 401	Mar. 12, 417
St. Zozimus	Greece	Mar. 18, 417	Dec. 26, 418
St. Boniface I	Rome	Dec. 28 or 29, 418	Sept. 4, 422
St. Celestine I	Campania	Sept. 10, 422	July 27, 432
St. Sixtus III	Rome	July 31, 432	Aug. 19, 440
St. Leo I (the Great)	Tuscia	Sept. 29, 440	Nov. 10, 461
St. Hilary	Sardo.	Nov. 19, 461	Feb. 29, 468
St. Simplicius	Tivoli	Mar. 3, 468	Mar. 10, 483
St. Felix III (II)	Rome	Mar. 13, 483	Mar. 1, 492
St. Gelasius I	Africa	Mar. 1, 492	Nov. 21, 496
Anastasius II	Rome	Nov. 24, 496	Nov. 19, 498
St. Symmachus	Sardo	Nov. 22, 498	July 19, 514
St. Hormisdas	Frosinone	July 20, 514	Aug. 6, 523
St. John I, Martyr	Tuscia	Aug. 13, 523	May 18, 526
St. Felix IV (III)	Sannio	July 12, 526	Sept. 22, 530
Boniface II	Rome	Sept. 22, 530	Oct. 17, 532
John II	Rome	Jan. 2, 533	May 8, 535
St. Agapitus I	Rome	May 13, 535	Apr. 22, 536
St. Silverius, Martyr	Campania	June 1 or 8, 536	Nov. 11, 537
Vigilius	Rome	Mar. 29, 537	June 7, 555
Pelagius I	Rome	Apr. 16, 556	Mar. 4, 561
John III	Rome	July 17, 561	July 13, 574
Benedict I	Rome	June 2, 575	July 30, 579
Pelagius II	Rome	Nov. 26, 579	Feb. 7, 590
St. Gregory I, the Great	Rome	Sept. 3, 590	Mar. 12, 604
Sabinianus	Blera in Tuscia	Sept. 13, 604	Feb. 22, 606
Boniface III	Rome	Feb. 19, 607	Nov. 12, 607
St. Boniface IV	Marsi	Aug. 25, 608	May 8, 615
St. Deusdedit (Adeodatus I)	Rome	Oct. 19, 615	Nov. 8, 618
Boniface V	Naples	Dec. 23, 619	Oct. 25, 625
Honorius I	Campania	Oct. 27, 625	Oct. 12, 638
Severinus	Rome	May 28, 640	Aug. 2, 640
John IV	Dalmatia	Dec. 24, 640	Oct. 12, 642
Theodore I	Greece	Nov. 24, 642	May 14, 649
St. Martin I, Martyr	Todi	July, 649	Sept. 16, 655
St. Eugene I	Rome	Aug. 10, 654	June 2, 657

APPENDIX

Name	*Birthplace*	*Accession*	*End of Reign*
St. Vitalian	Segni	July 30, 657	Jan. 27, 672
Adeodatus II	Rome	Apr. 11, 672	June 17, 676
Donus	Rome	Nov. 2, 676	Apr. 11, 678
St. Agatho	Sicily	June 27, 678	Jan. 10, 681
St. Leo II	Sicily	Aug. 17, 682	July 3, 683
St. Benedict II	Rome	June 26, 684	May 8, 685
John V	Syria	July 23, 685	Aug. 2, 686
Conon	unknown	Oct. 21, 686	Sept. 21, 687
St. Sergius I	Syria	Dec. 15, 687	Sept. 8, 701
John VI	Greece	Oct. 30, 701	Jan. 11, 705
John VII	Greece	Mar. 1, 705	Oct. 18, 707
Sisinnius	Syria	Jan. 15, 708	Feb. 4, 708
Constantine	Syria	Mar. 25, 708	Apr. 9, 715
St. Gregory II	Rome	May 19, 715	Feb. 11, 731
St. Gregory III	Syria	Mar. 18, 731	Nov., 741
St. Zachary	Greece	Dec. 10, 741	Mar. 22, 752
Stephen II	Rome	Mar. 23, 752	Mar. 25, 752
Stephen III	Rome	Mar. 26, 752	Apr. 26, 757
St. Paul I	Rome	May 29, 757	June 28, 767
Stephen IV	Sicily	Aug. 1 (7), 768	Jan. 24, 772
Adrian I	Rome	Feb. 1 (9), 772	Dec. 25, 795
St. Leo III	Rome	Dec. 26 (27), 795	June 12, 816
Stephen V	Rome	June 22, 816	Jan. 24, 817
St. Paschal I	Rome	Jan. 25, 817	Feb. 11, 824
Eugene II	Rome	Feb. (May), 824	Aug., 827
Valentine	Rome	Aug., 827	Sept., 827
Gregory IV	Rome	827	Jan., 844
Sergius II	Rome	Jan., 844	Jan. 27, 847
St. Leo IV	Rome	Apr. 1 (10), 847	July 17, 855
Benedict III	Rome	July (Sept. 29), 855	Apr. 17, 858
St. Nicholas I the Great	Rome	Apr. 24, 858	Nov. 13, 867
Adrian II	Rome	Dec. 14, 867	Dec. 14, 872
John VIII	Rome	Dec. 14, 872	Dec. 16, 882
Marinus I	Gallese	Dec. 16, 882	May 15, 884
St. Adrian III	Rome	May 17, 884	Sept., 885
Stephen VI	Rome	Sept., 885	Sept. 14, 891
Formosus	Portus	Oct. 6, 891	Apr. 4, 896
Boniface VI	Rome	Apr., 896	Apr., 896
Stephen VII	Rome	May, 896	Aug., 897
Romanus	Gallese	Aug., 897	Nov., 897
Theodore II	Rome	Dec., 897	Dec., 897
John IX	Tivoli	Jan., 898	Jan., 900
Benedict IV	Rome	Jan. (Feb.), 900	July, 903
Leo V	Ardea	July, 903	Sept., 903
Sergius III	Rome	Jan. 29, 904	Apr. 14, 911
Anastasius III	Rome	Apr., 911	June, 913
Landus	Sabina	July, 913	Feb., 914
John X	Tossignano	Mar., 914	May, 928
Leo VI	Rome	May, 928	Dec., 928
Stephen VIII	Rome	Dec., 928	Feb., 931

Name	Birthplace	Accession	End of Reign
John XI	Rome	Feb. (Mar.), 931	Dec., 935
Leo VII	Rome	Jan. 3, 936	July 13, 939
Stephen IX	Rome	July 14, 939	Oct., 942
Marinus II	Rome	Oct. 30, 942	May, 946
Agapitus II	Rome	May 10, 946	Dec., 955
John XII	Tusculum	Dec. 16, 955	May 14, 964
Leo VIII	Rome	Dec. 4 (6), 963	Mar. 1, 965
Benedict V	Rome	May 22, 964	July 4, 966
John XIII	Rome	Oct. 1, 965	Sept. 6, 972
Benedict VI	Rome	Jan. 18, 973	June, 974
Benedict VII	Rome	Oct., 974	July 10, 983
John XIV	Pavia	Dec., 983	Aug. 20, 984
John XV	Rome	Aug., 985	Mar., 996
Gregory V	Saxony	May 3, 996	Feb. 18, 999
Sylvester II	Alvernia	Apr. 2, 999	May 12, 1003
John XVII	Rome	June, 1003	Dec., 1003
John XVIII	Rome	Jan., 1004	July, 1009
Sergius IV	Rome	July 31, 1009	May 12, 1012
Benedict VIII	Tusculum	May 18, 1012	Apr. 9, 1024
John XIX	Tusculum	Apr. (May), 1024	1032
Benedict IX	Tusculum	1032	1044
Sylvester III	Rome	Jan. 20, 1045	Feb. 10, 1045
Benedict IX, 2nd time		Apr. 10, 1045	May 1, 1045
Gregory VI	Rome	May 5, 1045	Dec. 20, 1046
Clement II	Saxony	Dec. 24 (25), 1046	Oct. 9, 1047
Benedict IX, 3rd time		Nov. 8, 1047	July 17, 1048
Damasus II	Bavaria	July 17, 1048	Aug. 9, 1048
St. Leo IX	Egisheim-Dagsburg	Feb. 12, 1049	Apr. 19, 1054
Victor II	Dollinstein-Hirschberg	Apr. 16, 1055	July 28, 1057
Stephen X	Lorraine	Aug. 3, 1057	Mar. 29, 1058
Nicholas II	Burgundy	Jan. 24, 1059	July 27, 1061
Alexander II	Baggio (Milan)	Oct. 1, 1061	Apr. 21, 1073
St. Gregory VII	Tuscia	Apr. 22 (June 30), 1073	May 25, 1085
Bl. Victor III	Benevento	May 24, 1086	Sept. 16, 1087
Bl. Urban II	France	Mar. 12, 1088	July 29, 1099
Paschal II	Ravenna	Aug. 13 (14), 1099	Jan. 21, 1118
Gelasius II	Gaeta	Jan. 24 (Mar. 10), 1118	Jan. 28, 1119
Callistus II	Burgundy	Feb. 2 (9), 1119	Dec. 13, 1124
Honorius II	Fiagnano	Dec. 15 (21), 1124	Feb. 13, 1130
Innocent II	Rome	Feb. 14 (23), 1130	Sept. 24, 1143
Celestine II	Citta di Castello	Sept. 26 (Oct. 3), 1143	Mar. 8, 1144
Lucius II	Bologna	Mar. 12, 1144	Feb. 15, 1145
Bl. Eugene III	Pisa	Feb. 15 (18, 1145)	July 8, 1153
Anastasius IV	Rome	July 12, 1153	Dec. 3, 1154
Adrian IV	England	Dec. 4 (5), 1154	Sept. 1, 1159
Alexander III	Siena	Sept. 7 (20), 1159	Aug. 30, 1181
Lucius III	Lucca	Sept. 1 (6), 1181	Sept. 25, 1185
Urban III	Milan	Nov. 25 (Dec. 1), 1185	Oct. 20, 1187

APPENDIX

Name	Birthplace	Accession	End of Reign
Gregory VIII	Benevento	Oct. 21 (25), 1187	Dec. 17, 1187
Clement III	Rome	Dec. 19 (20), 1187	Mar., 1191
Celestine III	Rome	Mar. 30 (Apr. 14), 1191.	Jan. 8, 1198
Innocent III	Anagni	Jan. 8 (Feb. 22), 1198.	July 16, 1216
Honorius III	Rome	July 18 (24), 1216	Mar. 18, 1227
Gregory IX	Anagni	Mar. 19 (21), 1227	Aug. 22, 1241
Celestine IV	Milan	Oct. 25 (28), 1241	Nov. 10, 1241
Innocent IV	Genoa	June 25 (28), 1243	Dec. 7, 1254
Alexander IV	Anagni	Dec. 12 (20), 1254	May 25, 1261
Urban IV	Troyes	Aug. 29 (Sept. 4), 1261.	Oct. 2, 1264
Clement IV	France	Feb. 5 (15), 1265	Nov. 29, 1268
Bl. Gregory X	Piacenza	Sept. 1, 1271	
		(Mar. 27, 1272)	Jan. 10, 1276
Bl. Innocent V	Savoy	Jan. 21 (Feb. 22), 1276.	June 22, 1276
Adrian V	Genoa	July 11, 1276	Aug. 18, 1276
John XXI	Portugal	Sept. 8 (20), 1276	May 20, 1277
Nicholas III	Rome	Nov. 25 (Dec. 26), 1277.	Aug. 22, 1280
Martin IV	France	Feb. 22 (Mar. 23), 1281.	Mar. 28, 1285
Honorius IV	Rome	Apr. 2 (May 20), 1285.	Apr. 3, 1287
Nicholas IV	Ascoli	Feb. 22, 1288	Apr. 4, 1292
St. Celestine V	Isernia	July 5 (Aug. 29), 1294.	Dec. 13, 1294
Boniface VIII	Anagni	Dec. 24, 1294	
		(Jan. 23, 1295)	Oct. 11, 1303
Bl. Benedict XI	Treviso	Oct. 22 (27), 1303	July 7, 1304
Clement V	France	June 5 (Nov. 14), 1305.	Apr. 20, 1314
John XXII	Cahors	Aug. 7 (Sept. 5), 1316.	Dec. 4, 1334
Benedict XII	France	Dec. 20, 1334	
		(Jan. 8, 1335)	Apr. 25, 1342
Clement VI	France	May 7 (19), 1342	Dec. 6, 1352
Innocent VI	France	Dec. 18 (30), 1352	Sept. 12, 1362
Bl. Urban V	France	Sept. 28 (Nov. 6), 1362.	Dec. 19, 1370
Gregory XI	France	Dec. 30, 1370	
		(Jan. 5, 1371)	Mar. 26, 1378
Urban VI	Naples	Apr. 8 (18), 1378	Oct. 15, 1389
Boniface IX	Naples	Nov. 2 (9), 1389	Oct. 1, 1404
Innocent VII	Sulmona	Oct. 17 (Nov. 11), 1404.	Nov. 6, 1406
Gregory XII	Venetia	Nov. 30 (Dec. 19), 1406.	July 4, 1415
Martin V	Rome	Nov. 11 (21), 1417	Feb. 20, 1431
Eugene IV	Venetia	Mar. 3 (11), 1431	Feb. 23, 1447
Nicholas V	Sarzana	Mar. 6 (19), 1447	Mar. 24, 1455
Callistus III	Valencia	Apr. 8 (20), 1455	Aug. 6, 1458
Pius II	Siena	Aug. 19 (Sept. 3), 1458.	Aug. 15, 1464
Paul II	Venetia	Aug. 30 (Sept. 16), 1464	July 26, 1471
Sixtus IV	Savona	Aug. 9 (25), 1471	Aug. 12, 1484
Innocent VIII	Genoa	Aug. 29 (Sept. 12), 1484	July 25, 1492
Alexander VI	Jativa		
	(Valencia)	Aug. 11 (26), 1492	Aug. 18, 1503
Pius III	Siena	Sept. 22 (Oct. 1 (8)),	
		1503	Oct. 18, 1503
Julius II	Savona	Oct. 31 (Nov. 26), 1503.	Feb. 21, 1513

THE POPES

Name	Birthplace	Accession	End of Reign
Leo X	Florence	Mar. 9 (19), 1513)	Dec. 1, 1521
Adrian VI	Utrecht	Jan. 9 (Aug. 31), 1522	Sept. 14, 1523
Clement VII	Florence	Nov. 19 (26), 1524	Sept. 25, 1534
Paul III	Rome	Oct. 13 (Nov. 3), 1534	Nov. 10, 1549
Julius III	Rome	Feb. 7 (22), 1550	Mar. 23, 1555
Marcellus II	Montepulciano	Apr. 9 (10), 1555	May 1, 1555
Paul IV	Naples	May 23 (26), 1555	Aug. 18, 1559
Pius IV	Milan	Dec. 25, 1559 (Jan. 6, 1560)	Dec. 9, 1565
St. Pius V	Bosco	Jan. 7 (17), 1566	May 1, 1572
Gregory XIII	Bologna	May 13 (25), 1572	Apr. 10, 1585
Sixtus V	Grottammare	Apr. 24 (May 1), 1585	Aug. 27, 1590
Urban VII	Rome	Sept. 15, 1590	Sept. 27, 1590
Gregory XIV	Cremona	Dec. 5 (8), 1590	Oct. 16, 1591
Innocent IX	Bologna	Oct. 29 (Nov. 3), 1591	Dec. 30, 1591
Clement VIII	Florence	Jan. 30 (Feb. 8), 1592	Mar. 3, 1605
Leo XI	Florence	Apr. 1 (10), 1605	Apr. 27, 1605
Paul V	Rome	May 16 (29), 1605	Jan. 28, 1621
Gregory XV	Bologna	Feb. 9 (14), 1621	July 8, 1623
Urban VIII	Florence	Aug. 6 (Sept. 29), 1623	July 29, 1644
Innocent X	Rome	Sept. 15 (Oct. 4), 1644	Jan. 7, 1655
Alexander VII	Siena	Apr. 7 (18), 1655	May 22, 1667
Clement IX	Pistoia	June 20 (26), 1667	Dec. 9, 1669
Clement X	Rome	Apr. 29 (May 11), 1670	July 22, 1676
Innocent XI	Como	Sept. 21 (Oct. 4), 1676	Aug. 12, 1689
Alexander VIII	Venetia	Oct. 6 (16), 1689	Feb. 1, 1691
Innocent XII	Naples	July 12 (15), 1691	Sept. 27, 1700
Clement XI	Urbino	Nov. 23, 30 (Dec. 8), 1700	Mar. 19, 1721
Innocent XIII	Rome	May 8 (18), 1721	Mar. 7, 1724
Benedict XIII	Rome	May 29 (June 4), 1724	Feb. 21, 1730
Clement XII	Florence	July 12 (16), 1730	Feb. 6, 1740
Benedict XIV	Bologna	Aug. 17 (22), 1740	May 3, 1758
Clement XIII	Venetia	July 6 (16), 1758	Feb. 2, 1769
Clement XIV	Rimini	May 18, 28 (June 4), 1769	Sept. 22, 1774
Pius VI	Cesena	Feb. 15 (22), 1775	Aug. 29, 1799
Pius VII	Cesena	Mar. 14 (21), 1800	Aug. 20, 1823
Leo XII	Fabriano	Sept. 28 (Oct. 5), 1823	Feb. 10, 1829
Pius VIII	Cingoli	Mar. 31 (Apr. 5), 1829	Nov. 30, 1830
Gregory XVI	Belluno	Feb. 2 (6), 1831	June 1, 1846
Pius IX	Senigallia	June 16 (21), 1846	Feb. 7, 1878
Leo XIII	Carpineto	Feb. 20 (Mar. 3), 1878	July 20, 1903
St. Pius X	Riese (Treviso)	Aug. 4 (9), 1903	Aug. 20, 1914
Benedict XV	Genoa	Sept. 3 (6), 1914	Jan. 22, 1922
Pius XI	Desio	Feb. 6 (12), 1922	Feb. 10, 1939
Pius XII	Rome	Mar. 2 (12), 1939	1958

II

THE CARDINALS
Brief Biographies in Order of Seniority

EUGENE CARDINAL TISSERANT, a Frenchman, is the Prefect of the Sacred Congregation of Ceremonies and Dean of the Sacred College of Cardinals. In both capacities he is one of the most important persons during a Conclave, because this congregation regulates ceremonies to be observed in the Pontifical Chapel and Court, as well as the functions which the Cardinals perform outside the Pontifical Chapel. As Dean of the Sacred College and the Chief of the Cardinal Bishops (having the title of Bishop of Ostia), he places the tiara on the head of a newly elected Pope. This privilege of crowning the Pope has been accorded to the Bishop of Ostia since the fourth century. Cardinal Tisserant has another assignment, given to him by Pius XI in 1936. He is the Secretary of the Sacred Congregation of the Oriental Church; the Prefect (Chief) is the Pope himself. This congregation deals with all personal, spiritual, liturgical and other problems concerning that part of the Catholic Church which does not use the Latin Rite, and with all problems arising from the contact of the schismatic Orthodox Church, including the Russian Orthodox Church. (Born, 1884; created Cardinal, 1936.)

CLEMENTE CARDINAL MICARA, born in Frascati near Rome, was educated in the world-famous Pontifical Roman Seminary and later in the Capranica College. He received his higher education at the Gregoriana University and continued at the Pontifical Ecclesiastical Academy. He started his career as a diplomat very early. In 1909, he was Secretary of the Nunciature in Argen-

[139]

tina; in 1915, he became Uditore in Brussels. There, in Belgium, he helped to relieve the suffering population doubly oppressed by the horrors of war and occupation. His works of charity earned him the respect and the admiration of the Belgians as well as the occupational authorities. In 1916 he became Uditore in Vienna and in 1920 he was sent to Prague, where he remained until 1923 when he became nuncio for Belgium. Secular authorities, the hierarchy and the peoples of Czechoslovakia and Belgium remember with gratitude the tactful and understanding activity of this outstanding papal diplomat during the postwar years which were not easy in any European country. He remained in Belgium until 1940 when he was called to Rome but returned to Brussels in November 1944 at the end of the second occupation of the country. (Born, 1879; created Cardinal, 1946.)

GIUSEPPE CARDINAL PIZZARDO, almost eighty years old, is the Secretary of the Supreme Sacred Congregation of the Holy Office, highest office in the Curia. This is one of the three congregations of which the Pope himself is Prefect. The Holy Office, in dealing with all matters which directly or indirectly concern faith and morals, not only judges heresy and offenses that lead to suspicion of heresy but when it pronounces an adverse judgment, also applies the canonical punishment incurred by heretics and schismatics. The Holy Office decides whether or not a book is to be placed on the Index, makes a list of prohibited books, settles questions of mixed marriages and deals with matters of an alleged supernatural nature. Cardinal Pizzardo has spent all his life in the service of the Central Government of the Church dealing with these matters of highest importance. (Born, 1877; created Cardinal, 1937.)

BENEDETTO ALOISI CARDINAL MASELLA, a venerable sage, is the Archpriest of the Lateran Basilica. Although St. Peter's is important because the Prince of the Apostles is buried there, and because for hundreds of years canonizations and other great functions have taken place inside its walls, the Church first in importance for Catholics, the Church of the Pope, is the Lateran

Basilica. Cardinal Masella has served as nuncio in several countries. He had the privilege of crowning the statue of Our Lady of Fatima in 1946. (Born, 1879; created Cardinal, 1946.)

ADEODATO CARDINAL PIAZZA, one of the most venerable members of the Roman Curia, is a member of the order of the Discalced Carmelite Fathers, one of the most severe religious orders. He is President of the Italian Catholic Action and has great influence upon Catholic Action all over the world. His varied career includes two years of military service and long years of cloistered life during which he became, first, Prior of one of the important convents in Italy and, later, head of the order as Procurator General. He was Patriarch of Venice before being transferred to Rome. Now he is Secretary of the Sacred Consistorial Congregation. Extensively traveled, he was over seventy when he made a long tour of the United States. (Born, 1884; created Cardinal, 1937.)

FEDERICO CARDINAL TEDESCHINI, the only Cardinal who first was created *in petto* (Latin, *in pectore*). When the Pope nominates a Cardinal without at once proclaiming his name in consistory, it is because he finds it advisable to keep the selection secret. In such cases the Pope reserves the name of the Cardinal *in pectore* (in his breast) until he wishes to announce it publicly. Tedeschini became Cardinal *in petto* in 1933 and was proclaimed Cardinal two years later. From early youth he was educated in Rome and destined for service in the Government of the Church. He later served as nuncio and papal legate and now serves as Prefect of the congregation of the Basilica of St. Peter, of which he is also the Archpriest. The importance of St. Peter's Basilica is manifested in the fact that a special department (congregation) deals with questions pertaining to its upkeep and to the upkeep of all the buildings of the Vatican State. The people of Rome know Tedeschini intimately and call him the "Host of the San Pietro." (Born, 1873; created Cardinal, 1933.)

ALESSANDRO CARDINAL VERDE, priest since 1888, once the Secretary of the Sacred Congregation of the Rites, is a Cardinal who has never left Rome except for brief visits. His figure is closest to the imaginary one conjured up by people when they try to visualize a venerable old member of the Curia. (Born, 1865; created Cardinal, 1925.)

JOSEPH ERNEST CARDINAL VAN ROEY, Archbishop of Malines, Belgium, head of the Belgian, bilingual French and Flemish Church, is the spiritual leader of a deeply religious country. It is also a country which, largely because of the activity of its Catholic leaders, manages to reconcile advanced industrialization with proper social legislation. (Born, 1874; created Cardinal, 1927.)

PEDRO CARDINAL SEGURA Y SAENZ, once Primate of Spain, as Archbishop of Toledo was forced to resign his See during a period of religious persecution in his country. For him Catholicity and Hispanism are inseparable. A convinced defender of traditional forms of religiosity and government, he is respected by all despite divergent, prevailing views. (Born, 1880; created Cardinal, 1927.)

EMANUEL CARDINAL GONCALVES CEREJEIRA, Patriarch of Lisbon (Portugal), is the spiritual pastor of another small European nation with a great historical past, remembered for the achievements of its people as missionaries, sailors and discoverers. Now the whole nation is turned inward; its religiosity and simplicity are legendary and, since the apparitions at Fatima, Portugal has a new importance. Cardinal Cerejeira is reputed to be the embodiment of what is best in Portugal. (Born, 1888; created Cardinal, 1929.)

ACHILLE CARDINAL LIENART, Bishop of Lille, France, is a former soldier and officer in the French Army. Since priests were not exempt from military service, he participated in World War I, mostly at the front. An energetic man, he has performed near miracles in settling social questions in his diocese, which is rich in coal but was once ill-famed because of the misery of the coal miners. Lienart erected the Grand Seminary and the Cathedral in Lille. His sense of justice, his love of his fellow beings and his solid knowledge of social problems helped to create new social legislation in France. The French Christian Labor organization was started upon his initiative. The former captain, now a Prince of the Church, is a genuine labor leader. (Born, 1884; created Cardinal, 1930.)

PIETRO CARDINAL FUMASONI-BIONDI, Roman by birth, was Apostolic Delegate in India in 1916, then held the same post in Japan. In 1923 he became Apostolic Delegate to the United States and in 1926 assumed the same duties in Mexico. He is an expert on missionary work and church administration. For a number of years, when the missions field suddenly widened, he divided his duties with Celso Costantini. (Born, 1872; created Cardinal, 1933.)

MAURIZIO CARDINAL FOSSATI, Archbishop of Turin, Italy, comes from the ranks of priests who work in parishes. He worked God among the north Italians, industrial workers and small landowners for twenty years before he became Bishop. (Born, 1876; created Cardinal, 1933.)

ELIA CARDINAL DALLA COSTA, Archbishop of Florence, has been a shepherd of his flock all his life. From 1911 to 1923, he was pastor of an important industrial center in Lombardy, where people still remember him because of his work of charity among the poor and the destitute. In 1923 he became bishop of Padua and in this capacity he renewed the religious organizations and the entire religious life of his diocese, putting particular importance upon Catholic Action. In December 1931, Pius XI appointed him to be Archbishop in Florence and within a year he won the full cooperation of all the social strata of the diocese for his pastoral leadership. (Born, 1875; created Cardinal, 1933.)

THEODOR CARDINAL INNITZER, Archbishop of Vienna, a native of the former Sudeten belt of Austria where German and Czech population is in constant flux, knows intimately and from his own bitter experience the problems of this multilingual area of Central Europe. Himself a quiet scholar, he was called from the college classroom to head one of the oldest and most important dioceses in Europe. His archbishopric was practically behind the Iron Curtain for ten years while Vienna was surrounded by the

Soviets. (Born, 1875; created Cardinal, 1933; died, Oct. 9, 1955.)

IGNATIUS GABRIEL CARDINAL TAPPOUNI is the Syrian Patriarch of Antioch. Catholics of the Near East once were the strongest pillars of the Church and, though they have diminished in number because of schisms and heresies, their views and influence nevertheless are felt not only in Western liturgy but in the very essence of Western thought. Cardinal Tappouni is a native of an Arab country, Iraq, whose population in the main belongs to an extremist Moslem sect. Iraq recalls memories of Babylon and Assyria and, from recent history, of the country's embattled oil wells. Cardinal Tappouni is a representative of the millions of Eastern Catholics in the Sacred College. (Born, 1879; created Cardinal, 1935.)

LUIS CARDINAL COPELLO, Archbishop of Buenos Aires, is a reformer, a creative statesman and a priest of deep spirituality. He has built seminaries, reorganized the school system and religious education in Argentina and, for a number of years, was Chaplain General of the Army. He was thirty-nine years old when Pope Benedict XV appointed him Auxiliary Bishop of La Plata. Today he is a great sponsor and helper of youth and a fighter for religious freedom. (Born, 1880; created Cardinal, 1935.)

PIERRE CARDINAL GERLIER, Archbishop of Lyons, had a late vocation. He first studied law and became a lawyer and only when he was thirty-five years of age did he begin to study for the priesthood. He was forty-one when ordained. Seven years later he became Bishop of Lourdes and in 1937 Archbishop of Lyons and Cardinal. (Born, 1880; created Cardinal, 1937.)

 GREGORY PETER XV CARDINAL AGAGIANIAN, Patriarch of the Armenians, is spiritual leader of four million widely scattered people. A former parish priest from the Soviet Union, he was born in 1895 in Transcaucasia when the Tsar ruled over Russia. Agagianian's religious instructor recognized his exceptional gifts as a boy and the eleven-year-old Lazarus Agagianian was sent to Rome to study for the priesthood. In 1919, he returned to Georgia and became pastor of the Armenian Catholics of Tiflis. In 1922, he was called to Rome again and there he headed the Armenian Pontifical College. The Armenian Catholic Synod in 1937, following the death of Patriarch Arparian, elected him to head the Patriarchate. It was then that he took the names of Gregory and Peter. A part of the Armenian Church broke with the Vatican in the eleventh century; the patriarch's branch, however, was reunited with it in 1742. Though he is a Catholic Patriarch, he is considered the leader of all Armenians in the world. (Born, 1895; created Cardinal, 1946.) *DEAD*

EDWARD CARDINAL MOONEY, Archbishop of Detroit, was born at Mount Savage, Maryland. He was five years old when his family moved to Youngstown, Ohio, but he returned to his native Maryland when he entered St. Charles College at Ellicot City and, later on, St. Mary's Seminary in Baltimore. In 1905 Edward Mooney was sent by his superiors to Rome where he got his degree in philosophy and theology and where he was ordained in 1909. Immediately after his return to the United States he taught dogmatic theology at the seminary of the diocese of Cleveland, of which he became Rector in 1916. In 1922 he was appointed pastor of St. Patrick's Church, Youngstown, where he remained only one year. The brilliant young priest became spiritual director of the North American Pontifical College in Rome, the same college where he had studied before being ordained. His exceptional qualities, however, gave another direction to his life. In 1926, Pius XI appointed him Apostolic Delegate to India and elevated him to be Titular Archbishop of Irinopolis. He remained until February 1931 in India and his activity there was most successful. During these five years, eleven new missions were created in India and three dioceses were given into the care of the native clergy. It was during his stay as Apostolic Delegate that the Catholics of India erected a new building for the Apostolic Delegation, to commemorate the fiftieth year of ordination of Pope Pius XI. In February 1931, Msgr. Mooney was named as Apostolic Delegate to Japan where he worked with the same ability and success until 1933. In August 1933, he returned to the United States as Bishop of Rochester, N. Y., and in 1937, when the Holy See elevated the diocese of Detroit to an archdiocese, Msgr. Mooney became its first Archbishop. His activity as Archbishop of Detroit is too well known to enumerate all his achievements: the foundation of new parishes, chapels and mission centers; his care for religious instruction; his great social work. (Born, 1882; created Cardinal, 1946.)

JULES CARDINAL SALIEGE, Archbishop of Toulouse. He completed his ecclesiastical studies in the famous Parisien Seminary of St. Sulpice and was ordained in 1895. After getting his degree in theology at the Catholic Institute of Paris, he was Professor of Theology there for many years. In World War I he served four years as a military chaplain almost always in the front line. At the end of the war, he returned to his seminary in Pleaux and became its Rector. Consecrated Bishop in 1925 and Archbishop in 1928, Pius XI appointed him to the archdiocese of Toulouse. His sermons given in this city and in Paris are famous. He opposed any kind of chauvinism, promoted innumerable congresses to discuss social problems and questions of freedom. Being Grand Chancellor of the Catholic Institute of Toulouse, toward which the intellectual energies of eighteen dioceses of France converge, he is one of the great sponsors of ecclesiastical studies. During World War II, he was a firm and fearless defender of the rights and freedom of the people of southern France. His courageous attitude almost led to his arrest by the German occupying forces and the orders were changed only because of the serious illness of the Archbishop. (Born, 1870; created Cardinal, 1946.)

JAMES CHARLES CARDINAL MC GUIGAN, Archbishop of Toronto, Canada, studied in Quebec, and was ordained in 1918. He was first Chancellor of the Charlottetown diocese and in 1920 became secretary of the new Archbishop of Edmonton. Until 1930, his activity was concentrated in the Edmonton archdiocese, where he served first as secretary to the Archbishop, then as Chancellor and later as Vicar General. He founded in Edmonton the Seminary of St. Joseph and became its first Rector. In 1930, he was appointed Archbishop of Regina and in 1934 was made head of the archdiocese of Toronto. All his biographies point out his great administrative abilities. More important is his activity as pastor of the whole diocese. He founded summer schools for religious instruction. He increased the Catholic Church Extension Society in Toronto, he conducted campaigns for Catholic instruction in institutions of higher education. His Apostolic zeal is exemplary among his faithful. (Born, 1894; created Cardinal, 1946.)

SAMUEL CARDINAL STRITCH, Archbishop of Chicago, was born in Nashville, Tenn. He completed his studies at the Seminary of Cincinnati when he was sixteen years old and was sent to the North America College in Rome to finish his philosophical and theological education. He was ordained May 21, 1910, by Cardinal Respighi, Vicar of Rome. He returned to the United States and at twenty-four was made pastor in Memphis, Tenn. His exceptional abilities secured his rapid rise: appointed secretary to the Bishop of Nashville in 1915 and diocesan chancellor in 1917; in May, 1921, Benedict XV appointed him domestic prelate and in the same year Bishop of Toledo, Ohio. Thus, at thirty-four, Bishop Stritch became the youngest member of the Episcopate of the United States. He remained in Toledo nine years, marked by great activity. He built the new cathedral and erected many parishes and schools. In 1930, Pius XI appointed him Archbishop of Milwaukee where his great fame preceded him. The people of Wisconsin and especially of Milwaukee will never forget his helping hand during the years of the economic crisis. After the death of Cardinal Mundelein, Archbishop of Chicago, Pius XII appointed Bishop Stritch to succeed him. He took possession of his new See on March 7, 1940, in the presence of Archbishop Cicognani, Apostolic Delegate to the United States. The great qualities of Archbishop Stritch unfolded in an even ampler way when he became the leader of the most important diocese of Chicago. No problem escaped his watchful eye. He was deeply concerned with the social and educational problems of his diocese and of the whole nation. His activity later extended even into the international field because, by the consent of all the Bishops of the United States, he became Treasurer of the Bishops' War Emergency and Relief Committee. This committee raised the huge sums given by individual Catholics, i.e., by the entire Catholic population of the United States, to help ease the suffering of the victims of the war. It was one of the greatest and most efficient relief campaigns ever organized. Cardinal Stritch has been very active in the National Catholic Welfare Conference since 1935, as member of its Board. In 1939, he became Chairman of its administrative board which post he still holds. Despite this manifold activity, which was and is spent without publicity, Cardinal Stritch had time to publish his book *Principals for Peace* in which he presented to the American public the teachings of Pius XII and four preceding popes on international peace. (Born, 1887; created Cardinal, 1946.)

EMILE CARDINAL ROQUES, Archbishop of Rennes, was ordained in 1904. He received his superior instruction at the Catholic Institute of Toulouse. He also studied in Dusseldorf, Germany, to implement his formation as a future leader and educator of priests. Immediately after his return to France in 1906, he became Professor of Theology at the Seminary of Castres. For more than twenty years, he taught a whole generation of priests in the seminary and made his influence long lasting. In 1929, Pius XI appointed him Bishop of Mont-au-Ban and, in 1934, Archbishop of Aix, Arles and Embrun. In 1940, Pius XII elevated him to the archbishopric of Rennes. (Born, 1880; created Cardinal, 1946.)

CARLO CARMELO CARDINAL DE VASCONCELLOS MOTTA, Archbishop of Sao Paulo, Brazil, comes from a distinguished Brazilian family. He first planned to become a priest but left the seminary soon and decided to study law. For a while he was a distinguished civil servant. Here he felt his priestly vocation and returned to the seminary and completed his studies. He was ordained in 1918. For several years he was pastor in Bello Horizonte, then Rector of the seminary in the same city until 1932 when Pius XI appointed him Auxiliary Bishop. Three years later, in 1935, he became Archbishop of Maragnano where he remained nine years. His administration was so efficient that, upon his suggestion, the Holy See created two archdioseses from his one. In 1944, he became Archbishop of Sao Paulo and won the general esteem of the authorities and the population. He founded the Catholic Faculty of the University to fight the increasingly hostile attitude to the Church. He is known as a great educator and organizer. (Born, 1890; created Cardinal, 1946.)

NORMAN CARDINAL GILROY, Archbishop of Sydney, is a former soldier. He was the first Australian in the Sacred College. Born in 1896, he entered government service as a young man and became a telegraph operator in the Australian post office department. In 1914, he volunteered for the army, became an army radio operator and landed at Gallipoli with the famed ANZACS (Australia-New Zealand Army Corps) in the bloodiest battle of the Balkan peninsula. Wounded several times, he was sent back to Australia in 1916 and resumed his position in the postal department. In 1923 he was ordained as a priest and in 1934 was made Bishop. As papal legate, he several times visited Japan and India and was instrumental in helping to organize the first plenary council of the Catholic Bishops of India. (Born, 1896; created Cardinal, 1946.)

FRANCIS CARDINAL SPELLMAN, Archbishop of New York. The *Osservatore Romano* started an article about Cardinal Spellman in February 1946, when he was created Cardinal, with the following words: "He is one of the most eminent figures of the ecclesiastical world of our contemporary era." Cardinal Spellman was born at Whitman, Mass., and after graduating from Fordham University entered the North American College of Rome in 1911;

he was ordained in the Eternal City May 14, 1916. He received his diploma in Sacred Theology at the Propaganda Fide University of Rome. He then returned to the United States and for six years worked as a Chaplain in Roxbury and, later on, at the Cathedral of Holy Cross at Boston. In 1922, he became Vice-Chancellor of the Boston archdiocese and, in the same year, he entered the editorial staff of the *Pilot,* the diocesan weekly of Boston. Despite his great activity, he had time to translate two important books of the meditations of Msgr. Borgongini Duca. The year 1925 was one of the most important in his life because the young priest was called to Rome to serve in the Secretariat of the Vatican State. He remained there until 1932 translating the most important papal documents and radio messages of Pius XI into English. In Rome and at the Secretariat of State, he won many friends with his personal charm and hard work. In 1932 he became a member of the pontifical mission sent to the International Eucharistic Congress in Dublin, and in the same year the Pope appointed him Auxiliary Bishop to Archbishop O'Connoll of Boston. He was consecrated September 8, 1932, at St. Peter's Basilica by Cardinal Eugenio Pacelli, Secretary of State of the Vatican, later Pius XII. Msgr. Spellman became Archbishop of New York in 1939. A few months later, he was appointed Military Ordinary of the armed forces of the United States, a highly delicate and most important commission during the war years. Archbishop Spellman traveled thousands and thousands of miles across continents and oceans for the spiritual welfare of the members of the armed forces and, at the same time, of prisoners of war. His activity during and after the war for the welfare of his diocese, his constant concern for the problems of education, but particularly his energetic campaigns to help the victims of war brought him universal recognition. His literary works and his care for orphans are additional credits to him. "Such a prodigious activity, guided and maintained by solid preparation, by long and multiform experience, great physical strength and spiritual energy, are very seldom to be found in one person," says the *Osservatore Romano* about Cardinal Spellman. (Born, 1889; created Cardinal, 1946.)

JOSE MARIA CARDINAL CARO RODRIGUEZ, Primate of Chile, one of the most popular priests in South America, is called "the Bishop of the salt mines." His parents were destitute peasants in the village of Pichelmu on Chile's Pacific Coast. His health was so delicate when he was a young priest that doctors gave up hope. To strengthen him physically, his Bishop sent him to become pastor of the salt miners in the mountains. And not only did he recover physically but economically and socially he helped a whole exploited class of workers. (Born, 1866; created Cardinal, 1946.)

TEODOSIO CLEMENTE CARDINAL DE GOUVEIA, was born near Funchal on the island of Madeira, off the African coast. (Madeira is a Portuguese possession.) Cardinal de Gouveia is the son of an extremely poor family. He was the first native Archbishop of Funchal, then was transferred to Mozambique, Portuguese East Africa, and made first Archbishop of Lourenco Marques, capital of the colony. He is a man who cares for the interest of the hundreds of millions of Africans and is their voice in the Sacred College. (Born, 1889; created Cardinal, 1946.)

JAIME CARDINAL DE BARROS CAMARA, Archbishop of San Sebastian of Rio de Janeiro, Brazil, was born in 1894 and ordained in 1920. Already in 1925 his superiors entrusted him with the leadership of a very important seminary of Asambuja-Brusque. The young priest was so successful here, particularly helping the youth, that in 1928 he became canon and in 1935 domestic prelate. In 1936, Pius XI appointed him Bishop of Rio Grande do Norte. His activity embraced all strata of the population, but he directed his special interests to the workers and settlers of his large diocese. In 1941 he became Archbishop of Belem do Para and in 1943 Archbishop of Rio de Janeiro. (Born, 1894; created Cardinal, 1946.)

ENRIQUE CARDINAL PLA Y DENIEL, is the leading figure of the Spanish Episcopate, as Archbishop of Toledo and Primate of

Spain, and a great protector of religious freedom. As director of Catholic Action for all Spain he has had several occasions to express opinions on important matters, including the limits of the power of the state. (Born, 1876; created Cardinal, 1946.)

MANUEL CARDINAL ARTEAGA Y BETANCOURT, Archbishop of San Christophoro, Cuba, is the son of an old Cuban family which fought for national independence and has several times known exile. He is a great lecturer, preacher and defender of freedom of education. (Born, 1879; created Cardinal, 1946.)

JOSEPH CARDINAL FRINGS, Archbishop of Cologne, Germany, was born in 1887 and studied at the Universities of Innsbruck, Freiburg in Breslau and Bonn. Ordained in 1910 he was sent in 1913 to Rome to study in the famous Biblical Institute. At the same time he became Chaplain of the Santa Maria del Anima College, the national college of Germans in Rome. After his return to Germany at the end of 1914, he spent twenty-eight years as a chaplain and pastor in the archdiocese of Cologne. In 1942, he became Archbishop of the diocese. The new Archbishop was faced there with an almost insurmountable task. The horrors of the war hit Cologne daily. Almost the whole city went up in flames. Archbishop Frings suffered with his people and was the first to give help after each bombardment. Twice he remained buried under the ruins of buildings where he went to help people and was saved by the courage of his faithful. The figure of the Archbishop remains unforgettable to the people because during bombardments he put a helmet on his head and was seen running to bring aid. There is therefore an indissoluble tie between the Archbishop and his faithful; after the years of reconstruction it was tightened even more closely. (Born, 1887; created Cardinal, 1946.)

JUAN GUALBERTO CARDINAL GUEVARA, Archbishop of Lima, Primate of Peru, was the first Peruvian Cardinal to stress the growing importance of Latin America in the Universal Church. The faithful and the churches are extremely poor not only in Peru but in most South and Central American countries; nevertheless the ever-growing population, mostly Indians and mestizos, wants to keep its faith and its greatest need is priests. Cardinal Guevara was among the first Latin American Bishops who opened the doors for foreign missionaries, prominent among whom are Americans. (Born, 1882; created Cardinal, 1946; died, 1954.)

BERNARD CARDINAL GRIFFIN, Archbishop of Westminster, England, was born in 1899 in Birmingham, where his father, a well-to-do businessman and member of the City Council, gave much of his time to social work. He completed his studies at the King Edward's Grammar School and at the Cotton College in Staffordshire and during World War I he served as a military courier in the same city. After the war, he entered the Seminary of St. Mary of Oscott and afterward the brilliant young scholar was sent to study in Rome. He became a member of the Beda College while he studied at the Gregorian University. In 1924, in Rome, he was ordained priest. He returned to his country; his Archbishop, putting great confidence in the young priest, appointed him head of the Chancery and also his secretary. During this time, until 1937, he also worked intensively in the Catholic Evidence Guild. In 1937, he became director of a group of welfare organizations and, in 1938, after one year's work there, Pius XI appointed him Auxiliary Bishop to the Archbishop of Birmingham. After the death of the great Cardinal Hinsley, Archbishop of Westminster, Pius XII appointed Griffin as his successor. In 1946, when he was created Cardinal, the heir of the mantles of Newman, Manning and Hinsley, he was one of the youngest Cardinals. (Born, 1899; created Cardinal, 1946.)

JOSEPH CARDINAL MINDSZENTY, Archbishop of Esztergom, Primate of Hungary, is one of the great figures of the Church today. He was born in 1892, one of five children of a peasant farmer. His exceptional talent was discovered by his teachers in his early youth and, at the same time, his vocation for the priesthood became evident. With the help of his hard-working parents, and through the generosity of the Church, he succeeded in achieving his most cherished aim: to become Shepherd of

Souls. Joseph Mindszenty was a passionate pastor. He had no other interests as a chaplain, parish priest, Bishop and Cardinal than those of his flock, of his souls. He was ordained in 1915 and for almost thirty years, until 1944, he cared for those souls as chaplain and later as the pastor of a small but important southern Hungarian city. Even as a pastor, he carefully protected his parishioners from undue interference of any secular authority. It is significant that in one of his books he dealt with the personality of a Hungarian Bishop who was a champion defender of the rights and freedom of the Church. Mindszenty became Bishop of Veszprem in 1944 when his country was threatened by both Nazis and Communists. After the Nazi occupation of Hungary, he did not obey the Arrow Cross (Hungarian Nazi) authorities and he openly advocated that the senseless fighting should be abandoned. For his uncompromising stand the Nazis arrested him and sent him into the most severe penitentiary in the country. In 1945, after the death of Cardinal Seredi, Pius XII appointed him Archbishop of Esztergom and created him Cardinal in 1946. As early as 1945 Cardinal Mindszenty recognized that the Communists could not and would not compromise in their anti-religious attitude. He fought from the beginning for the freedom of the church, for freedom of education, freedom of press, freedom of assembly, freedom of self-expression and self-government. The Communists, recognizing that Mindszenty was their real foe, after a long campaign of intimidation, blackmail, and smear, arrested him and in a mock trial condemned him to life imprisonment. The Communists did not achieve their aim by silencing Mindszenty because his suffering strengthened the peoples behind the Iron Curtain and the outrageous trial branded those who engineered it. Cardinal Mindszenty was released from prison July 16, 1955, but still is not free at this writing. (Born, 1892; created Cardinal, 1946.)

ERNESTO CARDINAL RUFFINI of Palermo, Sicily, is a celebrated biblical scholar and educator. Under his direction, Catholic education was reformed all over the world. He became Archbishop of his Sicilian See in 1945 during the island's most difficult period, when riot followed riot and a whole society threatened to collapse. Cardinal Ruffini calmed the people and settled many problems, particularly by identifying himself with the destitute and the dispossessed. Ever since he has been the most popular man in Sicily. (Born, 1888; created Cardinal, 1946.)

ANTONIO CARDINAL CAGGIANO, the first Bishop of Rosario, Argentina, is a missionary himself of a diocese which came into being through a paternal care for the increasing population. His parents are poor Italian immigrants. He, however, was born in Argentina. (Born, 1889; created Cardinal, 1946.)

THOMAS CARDINAL TIEN, the first Chinese Cardinal, was born in 1890 in Ko-Chouang in the province of Shantung. His father taught Chinese for twenty-five years in various schools, and in 1897 became Professor of Literature at the Catholic Seminary of Po Li, and soon after was converted to the Church. Thus the young Tien was educated in the Christian spirit, and was baptized in 1901. He was not yet fourteen years old when he started his studies for the priesthood, and he was ordained in 1918. After several years of ministry he entered the Society of the Divine Word and practiced missionary work among his own people. In 1939, after serving as a Vicar Delegate, he was promoted to Apostolic Vicar of Yang Ku and was consecrated titular Bishop of Ruspe. In 1942 Bishop Tien became Apostolic Vicar of Tsing Tao. Because of the tragic events in China since the war, Cardinal Tien has not been able to return to his homeland. (Born, 1890; created Cardinal, 1946.) DEAD

CELSO CARDINAL COSTANTINI was born in 1876. He was ordained in December, 1899 and served, until the outbreak of World War I, as a chaplain. Very soon that part of northern Italy where he served became a war zone. Here he showed great ability to help people in desperate situations, to organize the protection of churches and of art. At the end of 1917 he asked to become a military chaplain. After the war he founded an association, "Friends of the Sacred Arts," and its magazine

Christian Art which is still being published as the leading Italian review for Christian art in Milan. He founded also an efficient and important institute to help the innocent victims of the war. In 1920, consecrated Archbishop, Pius XI sent him as the first Apostolic Delegate to China. His activity which lasted eleven years in China is called by his biographers unique. He organized in 1924 the first Chinese Plenary Council and it was during his term as Apostolic Delegate that the first native Chinese Bishops were consecrated. In 1935, he returned from China, leaving there a solidly organized and respected Church. In 1935, he became Secretary of the Sacred Congregation of the Propagation of the Faith. Very few persons with the exception of the popes have done more for the religious and cultural development and education of those territories where the faith struck roots recently. He published many books on the problems of China, on the missions, and on sacred art and is known all over the world as an expert on religious art. (Born, 1876; created Cardinal, 1953.)

AUGUSTO ALVARO CARDINAL DA SILVA is Archbishop of San Salvador of Bahia, Brazil. His administrative abilities, first as a pastor later as a Bishop, have helped Brazilian Catholics to stand firm during many stormy periods. (Born, 1876; created Cardinal, 1953.)

GAETANO CARDINAL CICOGNANI was born in 1881 and was ordained in 1904. From the very beginning of his studies at the Seminary of Faenza to their completion at the famous Pontifical Roman Seminary he was a brilliant student. He graduated in theology, philosophy, canon and civil law. Very soon, he became an official of the Rota and later Professor of Canon Law at the same Pontifical Roman Seminary where he studied. In 1912 he entered the Ecclesiastical Academy to prepare for papal diplomatic service. His career as a diplomat of the Holy See started in 1915 when Benedict XV sent him as secretary of the nuncio to Spain. From 1920 until 1924, he was Uditore of the nunciature of Belgium and at the same time chargé d'affaires of the nunciature of the Netherlands. In 1924, he was consecrated

Archbishop and sent to Bolivia as internuncio and later nuncio. At the same time he represented the Holy See at the celebrations of the first centenary of the independnce of Bolivia and he crowned the famous statue of the Virgin of Copa Cabana, the protectress of Bolivia. In 1928 he became nuncio in Lima, Peru, where he remained eight years. In 1936, he was named nuncio to Vienna and remained in this post until the Nazi occupation. In April 1938 Pius XI sent him as nuncio to Spain. (Born, 1881; created Cardinal, 1953.)

ANGELO GIUSEPPE CARDINAL RONCALLI, Patriarch of Venice, enjoys a distinguished record as papal diplomat, particularly in the Near East. He was first Apostolic Delegate to Bulgaria, then to Turkey and Greece, finally Apostolic administrator of the Latin Patriarchate of Constantinople, posts in which he dealt with the Orthodox branch of Christianity that broke away from Rome in the eleventh century. It was largely because of his friendly relations with the Orthodox that the Orthodox Patriarch sent a representative to the Coronation of the Pope in 1939, an event unique in its historical importance. As a nuncio to France after the liberation of Paris, he had the difficult task of pacifying spirits in a country that was spiritually torn. Besides being an eminent diplomat he is known as a distinguished historian. He wrote several detailed historical works about great personalities of the diocese of Bergamo, Italy, where he was born. Among his books, one about St. Charles Borromeo is of particular importance. (Born, 1881; created Cardinal, 1953.)

VALERIO CARDINAL VALERI was born in 1883 in northern Italy and finished his ecclesiastical studies and was ordained in Rome in 1906. From 1910 until 1920, he taught at the Diocesan Seminary of the northern Italian city Fano. During the war years and during the immediate postwar period, he was also active in welfare work, badly needed in those difficult times. In 1920, he was called to serve in the office of the Secretary of State of His Holiness where he rose rapidly. After a year in the Secretariat he was sent to Paris as Uditore, to the newly established nunciature. In 1927, Pius XI sent him as his Apostolic Delegate to Egypt. In that country he won the esteem of the non-Catholics too and his mission was so successful that the Holy See entrusted him with the leadership of the Apostolic Delegation to Palestine. In 1933 he became Apostolic nuncio to Bucharest, Roumania. In 1936 he returned to his first diplomatic post in Paris, at this time, however, as a nuncio. He remained in France until the end of 1944. During this time, he revealed an untiring activity to the benefit of the religious life of France. Before the Holy Year 1950, the greatest of all Holy Years recorded by history, Pius XII appointed him President of the Central Committee of the Holy Year. (Born, 1883; created Cardinal, 1953.)

PIETRO CARDINAL CIRIACI, a native of Rome, is a Church diplomat who served almost two decades in the Vatican's Secretariat of State, then became nuncio to Czechoslovakia and later nuncio to Portugal. Now he is the Prefect of the Congregation of the Council, the second oldest congregation, founded in 1564 to interpret and carry out the decisions of the Council of Trent. Throughout the centuries the congregation has become a sort of Department of the Interior; now it has authority over secular clergy and laymen as far as ecclesiastical discipline is concerned and over all questions concerning the observance of the commandments, as well as authority over pious and charitable societies. (Born, 1885; created Cardinal, 1953.)

MAURICE CARDINAL FELTIN, Archbishop of Paris, previously had governed three other French dioceses and comes from the ranks of country pastors. His predecessors, Cardinals Suhard and Verdier, were men and priests of exceptional spiritual and intellectual stature and were instrumental in revitalizing French Catholic life, recognizing the longing of intellectuals for a haven and the menace of new social revolutions. They acted in the spirit of freedom as taught by the Church and embraced also those who, although outside the Church, longed for the truth. Cardinal Feltin was faced with a practical side of the same problem, the worker-priest movement which seemed about to revolutionize the entire concept of Catholic priesthood. It was mainly Cardinal Feltin's wisdom that saved the situation. (Born, 1883; created Cardinal, 1953.)

MARCELLO CARDINAL MIMMI, Archbishop of Naples, started as a military chaplain, then served as Rector of a north Italian diocesan seminary. Before his appointment to Naples, he was Bishop of Crema in northern Italy, then Archbishop of Bari in the south where he created more than twenty new parishes and was instrumental in establishing labor movements and unions in an area where the population was helpless against economic exploitation and in danger of being misled by Communists. (Born, 1882; created Cardinal, 1953.)

CARLOS MARIA CARDINAL DE LA TORRE, Archbishop of Quito, Equador, is faced with great social problems in his homeland. Most of his faithful are Indians, so Cardinal de la Torre is a true missionary. (Born, 1873; created Cardinal, 1953.)

ALOYSIUS CARDINAL STEPINAC, Archbishop of Zagreb, Yugoslavia, whose martyrdom for his faith has been mentioned with that of Cardinal Mindszenty, was arrested in 1946 and sentenced to sixteen years in prison. Stepinac, a former soldier in the Austro-Hungarian Army, then an officer in the Yugoslav volunteer corps, several times seriously wounded in World War I, also spent two years in a prisoner of war camp. A graduate of an agricultural academy, he later managed his father's little estate and was late in finding his vocation. He started to study for the priesthood in Rome when he was twenty-eight and was ordained at thirty-four. Four years later Pius XI consecrated him as Bishop. For a while the Tito regime tolerated him, but Stepinac could not remain silent when churches were stormed, priests and laymen imprisoned and all individual freedom abolished. He protested and protested. As a result he was arrested and tried on trumped-up charges. Six years later he was released and confined to his native village. He was offered complete freedom if he would leave the country but, true to his oath, he refused. (Born, 1898; created Cardinal, 1953.)

GEORGES CARDINAL GRENTE, one of the great contemporary French scholars, was born in 1872. He is Archbishop-Bishop of Le Mans. Ordained in 1895, but continued his studies at the Sorbonne to complete his knowledge of classical and French classical literature. In 1914 he became Rector of the Catholic University of Lille and in 1918 became Bishop of Le Mans. Cardinal Grente published, among others, nine volumes of sermons and many books on history, about the Sacraments, about the popes. All his books had a vast echo in the literary world of France. He became in 1937 a member of the world-famous French Academy. He directs the work of the *Dictionary of French Letters.* (Born, 1872; created Cardinal, 1953.)

GIUSEPPE CARDINAL SIRI, Archbishop of Genoa, was born in 1906. At home he received not only religious instruction but an example of true Christian life as displayed by his parents. From 1916 to 1926 he studied in his native city. Then he was sent to Rome to complete his ecclesiastical studies at the Pontifical Gregorian University. He was ordained in 1928. In 1929 he graduated in theology *Summa cum Laude* and in 1930, in his twenty-fourth year, he became Professor of Dogma at the Seminary of Genoa. In 1931 he began his famous lectures for Catholic graduate students and his spiritual exercises for students and for the clergy. In a few years he became one of the intellectual leaders of Catholics in Italy, particularly through his lectures given to the leaders and assistants of the Italian Catholic Action. His two books *The Social Construction* and *A Course of Theology for Laymen* are famous. He was not yet thirty-eight years old when in March, 1944, Pius XII appointed him Bishop and named him Auxiliary to Cardinal Buetto, Archbishop of Genoa. His appointment was received with great enthusiasm, particularly among the humble of the population. He organized many campaigns and associations to help the destitute and the dispossessed by the war. After the death of Cardinal Buetto in 1946, he became Archbishop and his entrance to the city has been described as an "outbreak of joy" by the *Osservatore Romano*. Created Cardinal in 1953, the new Prince of the Church did not give up any of his intellectual social and educational activities and particularly that of being president and organizer of the Social Weeks of Italian Catholics. (Born, 1906; created Cardinal, 1953.)

JOHN FRANCIS CARDINAL D'ALTON, Archbishop of Armagh, Primate of all Ireland, is the 111th successor of St. Patrick. He was born in Claremorris in the archdiocese of Dublin in 1882. He finished his university studies at the Royal University of Dublin in 1904, then came to Rome as an alumnus of the Irish college. He was ordained in Rome in 1908, then returned to Britain to continue his studies at the universities of Oxford and Cambridge. In 1910, he graduated in Classical Literature from the National University of Ireland. In the same year he started to teach and taught Latin literature for twelve years at the National Seminary of Maynooth. After another fourteen years, he taught Greek Literature. In 1936 he became Rector of the same seminary and in 1941 Bishop of Meath. Five years later, in 1946, he was elevated to be head of the Metropolitan See of Armagh. Archbishop D'Alton, created Cardinal in 1953, traveled in many countries and was everywhere received as one of the most worthy representatives of the Irish nation, which for centuries has been most faithful to Christ and to His Church. (Born, 1882; created Cardinal, 1953.)

JAMES FRANCIS CARDINAL MC INTYRE, Archbishop of Los Angeles, was born in New York City. When he was eight years old he lost his mother, but despite such hardships of early youth he was determined nothing would prevent him from completing his education. After graduating from high school he studied at night and, after completing his courses, taught night classes himself at the City College of New York and Columbia University. At the same time he became a successful businessman, and was well established in 1915, when his father died. He decided, however, to leave the commercial world and study for the priesthood, a vocation which had attracted him since his youth. He completed his ecclesiastical studies in 1921 and was ordained by Archbishop, later Cardinal, Hayes in St. Patrick's Cathedral, New York. He became chaplain at the parish church of St. Gabriel, but after two short years Cardinal Hayes appointed him Vice-Chancellor of the Archdiocese of New York and in 1934 Chancellor. He has been a domestic prelate since 1936. In 1940 Pius XII appointed him Auxiliary Bishop at the side of the new Archbishop of New York, Francis Spellman. He was consecrated in 1941. In 1946 he became titular Archbishop and Coadjutor of Archbishop Spellman, who meanwhile became Cardinal. Pius XII transferred Archbishop McIntyre in 1948 to Los Angeles, and in 1953 the second Archbishop of Los Angeles became the first Cardinal of the Far West. His activities in New York are well remembered by all who worked with him. His untiring efforts in the educational field, his fight against the suppression of Catholic schools, are famous. In his new province he has created many new parishes, built churches and seminaries, keeping well ahead of an increasing population. (Born, 1886; created Cardinal, 1953.)

GIACOMO CARDINAL LERCARO, Archbishop of Bologna, was born at the Italian Riviera in 1891, son of a boatswain. He was the eighth of nine children. Three sons of this humble family became priests. He studied in the Diocesan Seminary of Genoa and was ordained in 1914. He completed his studies one year later in Rome at the Biblical Institute. During World War I, he served with the armed forces of Italy, mostly in the front line in the medical corps. From 1919 to 1923 he taught Holy Scripture and Patristics at the Seminary of Genoa and became member of the St. Thomas Aquinas College. During this time he gave lectures in religious questions for intellectuals. Later on, he started a movement in Genoa for the purpose of bringing a new religious spirit into the suburbs, the hospitals and the factories of Genoa. He became the first chaplain of the Apostolate of the Sea organized in Genoa. In 1937 he became pastor of one of the most populated parishes of the city. He particularly assisted families with numerous children and dedicated much care to the spirit of liturgy. During the most crucial periods of the war, which destroyed great parts of the city, his parish became a shelter for the poorest of the population with whom he even divided his meals. The Nazi authorities wanting to arrest him, he had to hide until the liberation of the city. In 1947 he became Archbishop of Ravenna, where he continued his social activity and dedicated special care to the devotion of the Madonna. He gave lectures and spiritual exercises all over northern Italy. In 1952, he became Archbishop of Bologna. About his activity in this city, *Osservatore Romano* writes the following: "The same evening of his entrance to the city, he started to visit one parish after the other. He is present at many important public manifestations and carries his word even to the most heterogenous audiences." A Swiss publication wrote about him: "In Cardinal Lercaro's archdiocese all but seven of sixty communes are under Communist administration, but he does not hesitate to take the charity and splendor of the Church boldly into the streets and factories." (Born, 1891; created Cardinal, 1953.)

STEPAN CARDINAL WYSZINSKI, Archbishop of Gniezno and Warsaw, Poland, a trusted leader of the Polish workers, stepped into the heritage of two great Polish Cardinals, Sapieha and Hlond, who both suffered as their nation did under the Nazis and the Soviets. The Polish Communist regime first tried to "make a deal" with the Cardinal, promising advantages which were allegedly to the Church's interest if it would remain silent concerning those ideals which eternally separate atheists and believers. When Wyszinski flatly refused, he was arrested. (Born, 1901; created Cardinal, 1953.)

BENJAMIN CARDINAL DE ARRIBA Y CASTRO, Archbishop of Tarragona, Spain, was born in 1896 as fourth of seven sons of a worker's family of modest means. He started his studies in Madrid, but later on was sent to the Spanish College in Rome to study

at the Gregorian University and the Biblical Institute. Returning to his country, he was called to teach at the Seminary of
Madrid, history, Greek and Hebrew languages and later on
fundamental theology. He became bishop in 1935. In his diocese,
he started an intense social activity among the workers. Particularly unforgettable are his famous Lenten sermons given to
the workers of the arsenal of Ferrol del Caudillo and to the
miners of Quenca Minera near Oviedo. In 1949, he became
Archbishop of Tarragona, where he continued his work among
the workers, among the youth and for the formation of an efficient clergy. (Born, 1886; created Cardinal, 1953.)

FERNANDO CARDINAL QUIROGA Y PALACIOS is the youngest among
the Spanish Cardinals and belongs to the five members of the
Sacred College who were born in this century. His year of birth
is 1900. Archbishop of Santiago of Compostella, he holds an important position in the religious life of Spain, inasmuch as this
city is the Sanctuary of St. James the Apostle, who is said to have
moved to the Iberian peninsula after the Ascension of the Lord
and began to Christianize the Iberians. His late successor is as
modern as St. Jacob was in his own time when Christianity meant
a real revolution of the soul. Quiroga y Palacios' first concern is
to help restore human dignity by adequate social reforms. (Born,
1900; created Cardinal, 1953.)

PAUL-EMILE CARDINAL LEGER, Archbishop of Montreal, Canada, was born in 1904. His biography says that his multiform
activity is tied to three continents: America, Europe and Asia.
He was born in Canada, received his ecclesiastical education in
Montreal and was ordained there in 1929. The same year he was
sent to France and in 1931 became Professor of Canon Law at
the Theological Seminary of the French capital. At the same
time, he was assistant master of the Novices of the Society of
St. Sulpice. His ability to organize and educate convinced his
superiors to send him to Japan where he founded, in 1933, the
Seminary of Fukuoka. For six years he educated future Japanese
priests in that institute. In 1939, he was invited to teach social

science at the Philosophical Seminary of Montreal. In 1947 he was called again to cross the ocean for a long period. He became Rector of the Pontifical Canadian College in Rome where he remained until 1950 when Pius XII consecrated him Bishop and appointed him successor of Archbishop Cardinal Villeneuve of Montreal. (Born, 1904; created Cardinal, 1953.)

CRISTANTO CARDINAL LUQUE, Archbishop of Bogotá, Colombia, was born in 1889, ordained in 1916. After fifteen years of parochial work, he became Bishop of Tunia in 1931 and he governed the diocese for eighteen years. In 1950, he became Archbishop of Bogotá. Msgr. Luque is well known in Latin America because of his interest in agricultural workers. He was one of the organizers of the National Federation of the Catholic Unions and gave much of his time to bring the thinking of his priests about social questions up to date. Another of his activities was and is Christian education. One of his specialties is the organization of courses through radio for the agricultural population. One broadcasting station beams a special program for peasants and farmers several hours every evening. This initiative caught the interest of UNESCO and most probably it will be adopted all over Latin America. (Born, 1889; created Cardinal, 1953.)

VALERIAN CARDINAL GRACIAS, Archbishop of Bombay, is the first Indian prelate who has been elevated to become a Cardinal. He was born in Karachi in 1900. At that time, Karachi belonged to the ecclesiastical diocese of Bombay. Now Karachi as well as Bombay are Archbishoprics. Valerian Gracias first went to the St. Patrick School in Karachi and later he was received into the Interdiocesan Seminary of Bangalore; from there he went to the Pontifical Seminary of Kandy (Ceylon). He graduated in theology with *Magna cum Laude* and was ordained in 1926. His first assignment was as a chaplain. He served at the St. Peter's Parish at Bandra (India), but later, in November 1927, he was sent to Rome to complete his ecclesiastical studies at the Gregorian University. In 1929 he returned to his country and remained for seven years secretary of Msgr. Lima, S.J., Archbishop of Bombay. Afterward he became ecclesiastical counselor of the Catholic Students Association, assistant in the diocesean branch of the Catholic Action, and administrator of the Diocesean Fund for the Clergy. For a while he belonged to the editorial staff of *The Messenger of the Sacred Heart*, later editor-in-chief of *The Examiner*, a monthly. In Bombay at this time, he published several books, among them: *The Vatican and International Policy*, *Heaven and Home* and *Features of Christian Life*. Pius XII named him Auxiliary Bishop to the Archbishop of Bombay and he was consecrated in June 1946. He became Archbishop of Bombay in December 1950. Cardinal Gracias is an excellent preacher and orator, besides being a real leader of the clergy and the faithful of India. (Born, 1900; created Cardinal, 1953.)

JOSEPH CARDINAL WENDEL, Archbishop of Munich and Freising, Germany, was born in 1901 as the son of a Bavarian tailor. He felt the priestly vocation in his early youth and it was Cardinal Faulhaber, at that time Bishop of Speyer, who helped the young man to achieve his aims. In 1921, he was sent to Rome to complete his studies at the German-Hungarian College. He was ordained in 1927. He graduated in philosophy and theology and returned to Germany in 1928 to become assistant pastor in Kaiserlautern. Later on he was director of the Catholic High School in Speyer. In 1938, he was appointed Director of Catholic charities in his diocese and in 1943 Bishop of Speyer. In 1952, after the death of the great Cardinal Faulhaber, he became the Archbishop of Munich and Freising. (Born, 1901; created Cardinal, 1953.)

NICOLA CARDINAL CANALI was born in 1874, son of Marchese Filippo Canali, and was ordained in the Holy Year of 1900. The brilliant young priest was an assistant of the Secretary of the Conclave of 1903 which elected Pius X. The Secretary of Conclave at that time was Msgr. Merry del Val, whom Pius X immediately appointed to be his Secretary of State. The young Msgr. Canali remained with Merry del Val and five years later was appointed to one of the important offices of the Secretariat, that of a substitute of the Secretary of State. He remained there until 1914. During this time, he had frequent important contacts with priests from all over the world, with Italian and foreign diplomats, and, as one of the organizers of the Italian Catholic Action, the whole strata of the local population. After the election of Pius XI, Msgr. Canali was offered one of the nunciatures but preferred to remain in Rome as an assistant of Merry del Val. As Secretary of the Sacred Congregation of the Ceremony, he worked and prepared the civil part of the protocol of the Pontifical Court. His activity in this respect became very important in 1925, which was a Holy Year. In 1926, Nicola Canali became assessor of the Supreme Sacred Congregation of the Holy Office where he worked with Merry del Val until the death of the latter. During the hard and difficult years of World War II, it was his task to guard the independence of the Vatican City. Cardinal Canali, as President of the Pontifical Commission for the tiny state of the City of the Vatican, acted wisely and made far-reaching decisions to protect the inhabitants of the small City and of Rome. As a faithful interpreter of the charity of the present Pope, he carried out the Pope's intentions to help the hungering and suffering population of Rome. Cardinal Canali is the Cardinal Penitentiary and patron of many religious orders. He worked with devotion in the canonization process of Pius X. (Born, 1874; created Cardinal, 1935.)

GIOVANNI, CARDINAL MERCATI is a veritable symbol of the priest-scholar. His present title is Librarian and Archivist of the Holy Roman Church and Protector of the Vatican Library. He has spent a long life in studies, particularly of documents and manuscripts. The Vatican Library is still growing and even now has the greatest and most important collection of manuscripts (about 70,000) and incunabula (6,836). It possesses about 700,000 printed volumes. Cardinal Mercati has worked all his life in the atmosphere of this library, which was built by Sixtus IV (1471–1484), the same Pope who built the Sistine Chapel. The whole personality of this scholarly Cardinal radiates history and tradition. (Born, 1866; created Cardinal, 1935.)

ALFREDO CARDINAL OTTAVIANI was born in 1890 in Rome. He started and finished all his studies in the Eternal City and was ordained in 1915. In 1926 he became Rector of the Pontifical Czechoslovak College in Rome. In 1928, Pius XI appointed him Subsecretary of the Sacred Congregation of Extraordinary Ecclesiastical Affairs. The next year he received the title of substitute of the Secretary of State. This was in 1929, the year that Italy and the Holy See signed the famous Lateran Treaty which re-established the Pope's secular sovereignty. Msgr. Ottaviani was very active in assisting Cardinal Gasparri who conducted all the negotiations with Italy. In 1935, he became assessor of the Sacred Congregation of the Holy Office and remained in this most important position for seventeen years. According to the *Osservatore Romano,* he played an important role in preparing the final report of the Commission of Studies which prepared the Dogma of Assumption. (Born, 1890; created Cardinal, 1953.)

III

THE PAPAL CHAPEL

All civilian and religious dignitaries who participate in the procession when the Pope enters St. Peter's Church to pontificate solemn Mass belong to the so-called Pontifical or Papal Chapel. Participation in the procession is strictly according to rank. The Papal Chapel thus has a liturgical function. Following are the members of the Papal Chapel in the order of their rank:

The Sacred College of Cardinals, Patriarchs, Archbishops and Bishops who have the title of Assistant to the Papal Throne

The Vice-Camerlengo of the Holy Roman Church

Two Italian Princes (Colonna and Orsini), Assistants to the Papal Throne

The Auditor General of the Apostolic Chamber

The Treasurer General of the Apostolic Chamber

The assessors and secretaries of the Sacred Congregations who are not Cardinals

The prelates of the Holy Roman Rota

The prelates of the Secretariat of State of His Holiness

Archbishops and Bishops who are not Assistants to the Papal Throne

Apostolic Protonotaries, whose title is given for life

Extraordinary Protonotaries

The prelate Commendatore di Santo Spirito

The Chief of the Roman Chancery

Abbots with the right to wear the mitre

General Abbots of the canons regular

General Abbots of the mendicant orders
Generals and Vicar Generals of the mendicant orders
The Master of the Saint Hospice
Prelate Auditors of the Rota
The Master of the Sacred Palace (Master of the Index, always
a Dominican)
Prelate Clerics of the Apostolic Chamber
Masters of the Pontifical Ceremonies
Participating Privy Lay Chamberlains
Nonparticipating Honorary Privy Lay Chamberlains
Consistorial Lawyers (Advocates)
Participating Privy Chaplains
Honorary Secret Chaplains
Privy Clerics of His Holiness
Procurator Generals of the mendicant orders
The Apostolic Preacher (always a Capuchin)
The Confessor of the Pontifical Family (always a member of
the Servite Order)
Procurators of the Apostolic Palaces
Sacristan of His Holiness
Altar Assistants at the Masses of the Pontifical Chapel
Pontifical Choir
Candlebearers
Clerics of the Pontifical Chapel
The Custodian of the Tiaras
Macebearers
Pontifical ushers

THE PONTIFICAL FAMILY

The Pontifical Family is the actual papal court. The following list, however, could create a false impression because of the number of so-called courtiers and because of their impressive titles. Actually only a few of them are in daily service of the Pontiff and the Vatican State. The rest of them are called only for solemn functions, such as receptions for foreign sovereigns, heads of states and diplomats.

1. Highest ranking members of the Pontifical Family are two Cardinals, the Cardinal Datary and the Cardinal Secretary of State, the so-called Palatine Cardinals.

2. The second group of the Pontifical Family is called the Noble AnteChamber of His Holiness and the members are:

a. The Palatine prelates: the Maestro di Camera; the Auditor of His Holiness; the Master of the Sacred Apostolic Palaces.

b. The participating secret chamberlains who actually perform daily service around the Pope. These are: the Master of the Alms; the Secretary of the Papal Briefs; the Secretary of the Cipher; the Office Chief of the Datary; the Secretary of the Latin Letters (Coppiere); the Secretary of the Embassies; the Guardian of the Papal Vestments; the Sacristan of His Holiness, who is also his vicar for Vatican City.

c. The Master of the Sacred Hospice.

3. The third group is composed of those civilian secret chamberlains who are actually in the daily service of the Pope and are called "secret chamberlains participant, *di Spada e Cappa*," *spada* and *cappa* meaning that they have the right to wear sword

and cape during solemn functions. These are: the Foriere Major of the Sacred Palaces; the Cavallerizzo Major of His Holiness; the Postmaster General; the Commanding General of the Noble Guard; the Commanding Colonel of the Swiss Guard.

4. The fourth group comprises the Assistants at the Throne (Patriarchs, Archbishops, Bishops chosen by the Pope); the Protonotaries; prelates of the Roman Curia.

5. The following make up the rest of the Pontifical Family:

Domestic prelates

All members of the Noble Guard

Secret Chamberlains

Honorary Chamberlains

The officers of the Swiss and Palatine Guards and the officers of the papal gendarmes

Privy Chaplains and Honorary Privy Chaplains

Nonresident Honorary Privy Chaplains

Privy Clerics

Ordinary Nonprivy Pontifical Chaplains

The Apostolic preacher

The Confessor of the Pontifical Family

Archiatro (physician) of His Holiness

His valet, called Aiutante di Camera

The quartermaster, called Decano di Sala

The Bussolanti

V

OUTLINE OF EVENTS DURING THE VACANCY OF THE HOLY SEE
and a
Brief Description of the Solemn Pontifical Mass and Coronation

THE FUNERAL, BURIAL AND MOURNING

On the first day following the day of the Pope's death.

The Pope's body is transported into the Sistine Chapel, put on a bier. For twenty-four hours the Penitentiaries of St. Peter pray at bier and Noble Guards mount guard.

Second day following the death.

Members of the Chapter of St. Peter's Church, accompanied by Cardinals and entire papal court, transport the Pope's body to St. Peter's Basilica to Chapel of the Most Holy Sacrament (on the right hand side of St. Peter's), where the Pope's body is on a catafalque (bier) exposed to public for at least twenty-four hours. Noble Guard mounts guard. Penitentiaries of St. Peter pray at bier.

Approximately the third day following death.

Bier with Pope's body is transported from the Chapel of the Most Holy Sacrament to the Apse of the St. Peter's Basilica. Pope's body is blessed and is put in three coffins, then lowered into vault.

Requiem Masses as held during this period at St. Peter's Basilica.

They are not celebrated at the main altar but at the altar at the end of apse, for nine consecutive days, by Cardinals. These Masses start first day after death of the Pope and end at ninth day following the death of the Pope. Masses are called novemdiali. (From Latin: nine days.)

Ninth day.

An official preacher designated by the Assembly of Cardinals eulogizes in Latin the deceased Pope in St. Peter's.

SEQUENCE OF EVENTS DURING PREPARATIONS OF CONCLAVE

The Vacancy.

On the day of the Pope's death:

His seal on the fisherman's ring is destroyed.

Camerlengo of the Holy Roman Church ascertains death.

Death certificate is prepared and sealed by Camerlengo and by one member of Apostolic Chamber.

Camerlengo takes over administration of Holy See and Vatican City.

Papal power rests; no encyclicals, bulls, briefs or any other decrees are issued.

Secretary of State loses office.

Sacred congregations perform only routine office work.

Cardinals outside of Rome are notified.

On the day after the Pope's death and on all following days up to the fifteenth day but not later than the eighteenth day following the death:

Cardinals arrive.

General Assembly of Cardinals meets each day.

Apostolic Chamber, under chairmanship of Camerlengo of Holy Roman Church, meets each day.

Camerlengo is assisted each day by three different Cardinals, rotating according to seniority.

Cardinals meet diplomats accredited to Holy See to receive condolences.

General Assembly of Cardinals appoints those whose presence is necessary at the Conclave (physicians, pharmacists, workmen).

APPENDIX

Marshal of Conclave in cooperation with Camerlengo prepares site of Conclave.

Arriving Cardinals swear into hands of Camerlengo that they will observe rules of Vacancy and Conclave.

From fifteenth to eighteenth day: Cardinals, each with two assistants and other personnel, enter Conclave.

THE CONCLAVE.

Voting.

Announcement of the election of new Pope.

THE CORONATION

Order of the papal procession.

The mendicant orders head the procession:

Discalced Augustinians

Friars Minor Capuchin

Minims of St. Francis de Paul

Mercedarians

Third order regular of St. Francis

Servites

Carmelites

Friars Minor Conventual

Friars Minor (Franciscans)

The Hermits of St. Augustine

Dominicans

Monastic orders:

Olivetan Benedictines

Cistercians

Benedictines of Vallombrosa

Camaldolite

Carthusians

Other Benedictines

Canons regular:

Canons of St. Norbert

[175]

Augustinian canons

Canons regular of the Lateran of Our Holy Redeemer

The following secular clergy:

A crossbearer and two acolytes

Students of the Pontifical Roman Seminary

All pastors of the Parish Churches of Rome

Dignitaries and canons of the Collegiate and Basilica Churches of the City, with their respective clergy in the following order:

Collegiate Churches:

St. Anastasia

St. Celsus and Julian

St. Eustace

Our Lady in Via Lata

St. Nicholas in Carcere

St. Mark

The Holy Angel in Pescheria

St. Lawrence in Lucina

Minor Basilicas:

Our Lady Queen of Heaven in Monte Sacro

St. Mary in Cosmedin

St. Mary in Trastevere

St. Lawrence in Damaso

Patriarchal Basilicas:

St. Mary Major

St. Peter

St. John Lateran

The Vicegerent of Rome with members of the vicariate (The Vicegerent is the Vicar of the Cardinal Vicar).

The Papal Court:

Two members of the Swiss Guard

Chamberlains of Honor, Supernumerary
Chamberlains of the Cape and Sword } Laymen

The College of Procurators of the Apostolic Palaces

The Capuchin Apostolic Preacher

The Servite Confessor of the Papal Household
Macebearers
The Common Chaplains
The Privy Clerics
The Honorary Privy Chaplains
The Consistorial Advocates
The Honorary and Supernumerary Privy Chamberlains
The Privy Chamberlains Participant
The Referendaries of the Segnatura and with them the Assistant Priest, Deacon and Subdeacon of the Papal Chapel
The Votaries (Judges) of the Segnatura
The Clerics of the Apostolic Chamber
Two Apostolic Couriers
The Auditors (Judges) of the Sacred Rota
The Master of the Sacred Palace (Dominican)
Two Privy Chaplains carrying the tiara and mitre which are to be used by the Pope
The Grand Master of the Sacred Hospice
The clergy in sacred vestments are headed by the Dean of the Segnatura carrying the thurible, accompanied by the junior of the Auditors of the Rota acting as Apostolic Subdeacon. They are surrounded by seven Votaries of the Segnatura as acolytes who carry seven candlesticks with ornamental candles.
Abbots in their own right
Mitred Abbots General
Monsignor Commendatore of the Santo Spirito
Penitentiaries of St. Peter's carrying long rods, garlanded with flowers
Bishops
Archbishops
Patriarchs
Cardinal Deacons
Cardinal Priests
Cardinal Bishops
The Prince Assistant at the Papal Throne

Vice-Camerlengo of the Holy Roman Church
Two Cardinal Deacons who will remain at the throne
Two Auditors of the Rota to hold the *falda*
Two Cardinals who will assist the Pope at Mass
The two first Masters of Ceremonies
His Holiness on the Sedia Gestatoria, carried by *sediari*
The canopy is carried by various personages of the Pontifical Chapel
The flabelli (ostrich fans) are carried by two Privy Chamberlains
Behind the Pope:
> The Dean of the Rota, walking between two Privy Chamberlains
> The Archiatro, the Physician of His Holiness
> The Personal Valet of His Holiness
> The College of Protonotaries Apostolic
> The other Supernumerary Chamberlains, Chaplains, Clerics
Lastly:
> Generals of the Religious Orders
> Bussolanti
> Ushers

When the procession enters the portico (that space which is between the heavy gates of a church and the church proper; the portico of St. Peter's is as long as the façade of St. Peter's and about twenty-five yards wide), it stops.

The Pope descends from the *sedia gestatoria* and mounts a canopied throne. The Pope, there, receives expression of reverence by Cardinals and the clergy of St. Peter's Church.

The Pope then mounts *sedia gestatoria* again and is carried into St. Peter's Basilica proper. He is carried to a side chapel at the righthand side of the Basilica; this is the Chapel of the Holy Sacrament. There he descends from *sedia gestatoria* and prays inside the chapel.

Then the Pope remounts *sedia gestatoria* and is carried to the Chapel of St. Gregory. Here he sits on the prepared throne. He is vested here after the prayers of the Divine Office (see text).

The red velvet shoes of the Pope are taken off and buskins and sandals of embroidered white silk are put on. The color of the buskins and the sandals is determined by the liturgical color of the day. Then the gremial veil is placed upon the Pope's knees to protect his vestments. The Prince Assistant to the Throne pours water over the Pope's hands and a private cleric hands him a towel. Liturgical reason for handwashing is cleansing; materially as well as spiritually. Then a Cardinal takes off the mitre from the Pope's head, and also the white or red stole (according to the liturgical color of the day); he then vests the Pontiff in the sacred vestments necessary for the Mass.

First he puts the succinctorium or cord interlaced with gold on the Pope. The succinctorium replaces the girdle which is worn over the alb. The succinctorium's ends are large and flat and represent the ancient alms purse which the popes wore. This purse was full of money which the Pope distributed wherever he went. The custom is abolished but the succinctorium, as its symbol, remained.

After this the Cardinal puts the pectoral cross (see text) and the tippet [*fanone*] on the Pope. The tippet is a vestment worn only by the Pope. It is a double cape; the upper part of it is the shorter part. It is made of silk embroidered with gold and placed over the alb and the stole. The upper part is raised until the Pope is vested in dalmatic and chasuble and then allowed to fall so as to resemble a mozzetta (see text).

The Cardinal puts the mitre on the Pope's head, and then the ring. This is not the fisherman's ring; it is the ring pertaining to the Pope as Bishop of Rome. Then another Cardinal hands the Pope the incense boat which he blesses and puts incense in the thurible.

After the Pope is vested and mounts the *sedia gestatoria,* the procession continues to the main altar.

While going to the main altar, the procession is stopped three times and the Pope is reminded that all this glory is not his at the ceremony of the burning of the flax.

THE PONTIFICAL MASS

The Mass begins. The Pope is at the steps of the altar and says the first prayers and the *Confiteor*. Then he steps up to the altar, kisses the altar and kisses the Book of Gospels. Then the Pope incenses the altar. After this, he leaves the altar and goes to the throne. Here his mitre is removed and he recites the *Kyrie*, and later intones the *Gloria in excelsis Deo*. Then the mitre is placed upon his head, he sits down, and the gremial veil is put upon his knees. When the singing of the *Gloria* is ended the Pope's mitre is removed, he stands up, then he sings *Pax Vobis* and the Collect, after which he sits again. Then, after the Epistle is sung in Greek by a priest of the Greek College and in Latin by the Cardinal Latin Subdeacon, the Pope reads the Epistle, Gradual and Gospel half loudly at the throne.

When he finishes the reading of the Gospel, first the Latin Book of Gospels is brought to him which he incenses, blesses and kisses. The Pope remains at the throne, a Cardinal Deacon goes to the Gospel side of the altar and sings the Gospel in Latin.

When the Latin Gospel is ended, a monk of the Greek Catholic order of St. Basil takes the Greek Book of Gospels to the Pope, who blesses, incenses and kisses it. The Pontiff remains at the throne, the monk with the Greek Book of Gospels goes to the altar and exclaiming in ancient Greek, "*Sophia*" (Wisdom), sings the Gospel in Greek. Then both Latin and Greek Books of the Gospels are carried to the Pope who kisses them. The Pope is incensed.

After the singing of the *Credo* during which all sit, follows the testing of the wine and water. The officiating Cardinals go to the Sacristy (or credence) tables at the side of the main altar, purify the chalice, paten, golden spoon, and the wine cruet with wine, the water cruet with water. The cupbearer, a Bishop, then tastes

wine and water to show that they do not contain dangerous sub-
stance. Then he (the cupbearer) consumes two Hosts (not consecrated yet) while turning toward the Pope. The third Host will
be used for the Mass. Then he drinks the wine and water immediately (the same wine and water which he tasted a few minutes before).

The Pope's gloves and his skullcap are removed. After this
ceremony is finished the Pope washes his hands, assisted by the
prince assistant to the throne, and proceeds to the altar.

The Pope offers the Host on the paten, staying at the middle
of the altar as in any Low Mass.

Then a Cardinal pours wine, enough for three celebrants, into
the chalice and another Cardinal pours water into a golden
spoon which he offers the Pope and the Pope blesses it. Then the
blessed water from the spoon is poured into the chalice and given
to the Pope, who stays at the middle of the altar and offers (lifts
up) the chalice with the paten, as in any Low Mass.

The Pope, at the altar, incenses the wine and the Host, then
he is incensed.

The Pope then washes his hands at the Epistle side of the altar
as in any other Mass and returns to the middle of the altar where
he continues the prayers of the Mass and sings the *Preface*.

At the *Sanctus* eight prelates carrying lighted torches kneel in
front of the altar.

The Pope recites the canon at the altar. The choir in the
meantime sings the *Sanctus*. Afterward everybody kneels in
silence.

The Pope at the altar pronounces the words of Consecration
first upon the Host, then upon the chalice with the wine. He
elevates both Host and chalice, first, as every priest does, in the
middle of the altar, then toward right and left, to show it to
everybody. This is a privilege of the Pope. Then the Pope begins
the Lord's Prayer (*Pater Noster*), still at the altar.

Then His Holiness breaks the Sacred Host. The Pope at the
altar sings *Pax Domini sit semper vobiscum,* then he says the

Agnus Dei and the first of the prayers before the Communion which begins with *"Domine Jesu Christe."* The Pope then kisses the altar and embraces two assisting Cardinals. He genuflects before the Sacred Host and the chalice containing the Precious Blood; with head uncovered and hands joined, the Pope returns from the altar to the throne.

The Sacred Host then is brought to the Pope with great ceremony (at the throne) and he takes one of the two halves of the Sacred Host in his left hand and says *"Panem celestem accipiam"* ("I will accept the celestial bread") then strikes three times his breast saying *"Domine non sum dignus"* ("Lord, I am not worthy") and makes the sign of the Cross with the Host, saying: *"Corpus Domini Jesu Christi custodiat me ad vitam aeternam Amen."* "May the body of Our Lord Jesus Christ keep my soul unto life everlasting. Amen.") Then the chalice with the Precious Blood is brought to the Pope with the golden tube; he puts this into the chalice in order to drink a portion of the Precious Blood after having said: *"Calicem salutaris accipiam."* ("I will take the chalice of salvation.") After this the Pope gives Communion to the assisting Cardinals with the Apostolic Subdeacon (of the Rota) also assisting.

The Pope is still at the throne. Another chalice is brought to him and the chalice with the Precious Blood; he purifies the latter chalice. The Pope takes the last remnants out of the chalice and then washes his hands.

After this the Pope leaves the throne, returning to the altar where he reads the Communion and sings the *Postcommunion.* The *Ita Missa Est* is sung by one of the Cardinals.

Thereafter, the Pope goes to the Gospel side of the altar and reads the Last Gospel, after which the mitre is replaced upon his head.

At the end of the Mass the Pope mounts the *sedia gestatoria.*

Between main altar and Holy Sacrament Chapel, the procession is stopped by the Archpriest Cardinal of St. Peter's who gives the Pope on *sedia gestatoria* a white silken purse embroid-

ered with gold. The purse contains twenty-five julies, the coins of
Pope Julius II. These same coins are always presented to the
Pope. Afterward, the train bearer of one of the Cardinals (to
whom the Pope hands over the purse) takes them back to the
Sacristan of the Basilica (a high prelate) and receives their mod-
ern equivalent in exchange. The meaning of this ceremony: Since
St. Peter's is not the Pope's (Bishop of Rome) own church, at the
end of the Divine Service the Archpriest of St. Peter's expresses
his gratitude for the *"Missa ben cantata"*—for the "well sung
Mass."

The Pope is taken to the Chapel of the Most Holy Sacrament.

Then, in *sedia gestatoria*, the Pope is carried out onto the
balcony of St. Peter's.

The Coronation takes place on the balcony and is viewed by
the crowds assembled in the great plaza in front of the Basilica.

VI

BUILDINGS IN ROME BELONGING TO THE HOLY SEE BUT OUTSIDE OF THE VATICAN

All the buildings listed below enjoy extraterritorial rights, i.e., they are the sovereignty of the Vatican and not the Italian State. No Italian official may enter them without permission and no Italian authority (police, treasury, etc.) has any right within them. The buildings are:

The Lateran Basilica and the Lateran Palace, with the so-called Holy Stairway (Scala Santa)

The St. Mary Major Basilica

The St. Paul Basilica *fuori lemura,* i.e., outside of the city walls of Rome

The Papal Palace and the whole estate in the village of Castel Gandolfo in the neighborhood of Rome

The Palace of the Datary

The Palace of the Cancelleria

The Palace of the Congregation for the Propagation of the Faith

The San Callisto Palace

The Palace of the Sacred Congregation of the Oriental Rites

The Palace of the Sacred Congregation of the Holy Office

The Palace of the Vicariate of Rome

All the buildings belonging to the Holy See on the Janiculum Hill, with all the institutes under the jurisdiction of the Propagation of the Faith

The following buildings belonging to the Holy See have no

extraterritorial rights, but the Italian Government cannot expropriate them and they are tax-exempt:

The Gregorian University

The Biblical Institute

The Palace connected with the Basilica "Twelve Apostles"

The Palace connected with the San Carlo Church at the "Corso"

The following buildings which are connected with one another:

The Archeological Institute

The Oriental Institute

The Lombardy College

The Russian Institute

The St. Apollinaris Palace

The retreat house for clergy connected with the Church St. John and Paul

VII

ECCLESIASTICAL INSTITUTIONS IN ROME

The following are the major ecclesiastical institutions in Rome. The seminaries, like theological seminaries all over the world, prepare students for the priesthood. The colleges are institutions for students of theology and for already ordained priests sent there by their Bishops for higher education. To become a member of a Roman seminary or college is a great privilege. The students or priests receive room and board, are under strict ecclesiastical supervision and study at one of the pontifical universities. They wear distinctive dress. Members of one college wear red cassock, of another blue, of another purple, and so on.

Seminaries are: Collegio Romano; Collegio Romano for Law Studies; St. Louis, King of France, French Seminary; St. Ambrose and Charles Seminary for Lombardy.

Colleges: North American; Armenian; St. Beda College for English Converts who study for the Catholic priesthood; Belgian; Canadian; Capranica (four hundred years old, the most venerated Roman college); Ethiopian (Abyssinian); German-Hungarian; Greek; English; Irish; Maronite (Oriental Rites); St. John Nepomuk (Czechoslovak); Dutch; Brazilian; Latin-American; Roumanian; Polish; Portuguese; Russian; Ruthenian (Ukrainian); College of the Priests for Italian Emigration; Illyric (Crotian); St. Mary of the Lake (it belongs to the diocese of Chicago); Scottish; Spanish; Teutonic of Santa Maria dell' Anima (German); Teutonic of Santa Maria in Campo Santo (German); the Urban College of the Propagation of the Faith; Polish Ecclesiastical Institute; Hungarian Ecclesiastical Institute.

APPENDIX

In addition to the above there are forty-four colleges belonging to various religious orders.

Institutes of Graduate Studies: Pontifical Gregorian University; Pontifical Lateran Atheneum; Pontifical Atheneum of the Urban College "de Propaganda Fide"; Pontifical International Institute of "Angelicum"; Pontifical International Institute of St. Anselm; Atheneum Antonianum; Pontifical Institute of Sacred Music; Pontifical Institute of Christian Archeology.

VIII

ORGANIZATION AND HIERARCHY OF THE CHURCH

A PRIEST in the Roman Catholic Church is a minister of divine worship who is ordained by a bishop in union with the Pope. Through his ordination he receives authority to offer the highest act of divine service, the Sacrifice of the Mass. He is empowered to baptize, to administer Extreme Unction and, having jurisdiction, administer the Sacrament of Penance (hear confessions), assist in the Sacrament of Matrimony and, with special permission, administer the Sacrament of Confirmation. An ordained priest is a priest of the second order.

A BISHOP is a priest of the first order; he can administer all the above mentioned sacraments and the Sacrament of Holy Order— i.e., he can ordain priests and consecrate other bishops. Bishops are the successors of the Apostles and govern the diocese. A titular bishop is a full bishop appointed to a diocese that exists only nominally.

AN ARCHBISHOP is a bishop who has authority, properly defined, over an ecclesiastical province (a territorial division usually including one or more dioceses).

A PATRIARCH is a bishop, highest in rank below the Pope in jurisdictional affairs. The patriarchs are not subject to any ecclesiastical authority but the Pope and his legates.

The hierarchy of the Church consists of Minor Orders and Major Orders. Those who prepare for the priesthood receive during their studies the following Minor Orders, all having meaning in the liturgy of the Church: Porter, Reader, Exorcist, Acolyte. The Major Orders are: Subdeacon, Deacon, Priest, Bishop (Archbishop, Patriarch).

APPENDIX

PRELATES are real and titular, both meaning a papal distinction. Generally a bishop is also called a prelate.

CARDINALS are treated on page 139.

CONSISTORIES are assemblies of Cardinals called together by the Pope and presided over by him.

COUNCILS are assemblies of prelates summoned by their lawfully appointed chief. There are diocesan councils (synods) called by the bishop; provincial councils consisting of a meeting of the bishops of a province; plenary or national councils consisting of the meeting of the episcopate of a country or region under the chairmanship of the Pope's emissary (legate).

The GENERAL or ECUMENICAL COUNCIL is an assembly of all bishops of the world called together by the Pope. The last Ecumenical Council was opened in 1869 by Pope Pius IX. It was adjourned in 1870, but not closed. All decisions of any council are subject to the approval of the Pope.

The ROMAN CURIA consists of churchmen organized into various groups in order to aid in the government of the Church. Since he is absolute sovereign in all matters of the Church, the Pope delegates some of his jurisdiction to these groups. The Curia consists of:

1. The Sacred Congregations:
   Supreme Sacred Congregation of the Holy Office
   Sacred Consistorial Congregation
   Sacred Congregation for the Oriental Church
   Sacred Congregation of the Sacraments
   Sacred Congregation of the Council
   Sacred Congregation of Religious
   Sacred Congregation for the Propagation of the Faith
   Sacred Congregation of Rites
   Sacred Congregation of Ceremonies
   Sacred Congregation of Extraordinary Ecclesiastical Affairs
   Sacred Congregation of Seminaries and Universities
   Sacred Congregation of the Basilica of St. Peter.

2. Tribunals:

   Sacred Apostolic Penitentiary
   Supreme Tribunal of the Apostolic Signature
   Sacred Roman Rota

3. Offices:

   Apostolic Chancery (Cancelleria)
   Apostolic Datary
   Apostolic Camera
   Secretariate of State
   Secretariate of Briefs to Princes and Latin Letters

4. Modern Popes, particularly Pius XII, created pontifical commissions to cope with the ever increasing need of organizational and other problems of our age. Permanent commissions are:

   Commission of Biblical Studies
   Commission for the Authentic Interpretation of the Code of Canon Law
   Commission for the Redaction of the Oriental Code of Canon Law
   Abbacy of Saint Jerome for the Revision and Emendation of the Vulgate (Acting as Pontifical Commission)
   Commission of Sacred Art in Italy
   Commission for Motion Pictures
   Commission for the Care of the Pontifical Sanctuary of Pompei
   Commission for the Preservation of the Faith and for the Provision of New Churches in the City of Rome
   Commission for the Care of the Historical and Artistic Monuments of the Holy See
   Commission of Heraldry for the Pontifical Court
   Commission for Assistance and Welfare
   Commission for Russia
   Commission for the Government of Vatican City
   Commission for the Administration of the Mobile and Immobile Possessions of the Holy See

APPENDIX

5. Papal Diplomacy:

Papal legates represent him at specific occasions and functions

Nuncios are diplomatic representatives of the Pope at foreign governments

Internuncios are nuncios of lower rank

Apostolic Delegates are representatives of the Holy See (The Pope) at the Hierarchy (episcopate) of a country which has no diplomatic relations with the Holy See

IX

DIPLOMATIC RELATIONS OF THE VATICAN

The Holy See has nuncios or internuncios accredited to the governments of the following countries:

Argentina, Austria, Belgium, Bolivia, Brazil, Chile, China (Nationalist), Colombia, Costa Rica, Cuba, Dominican Republic, Ecuador, Egypt, El Salvador, France, Germany, Guatemala, Haiti, Honduras, India, Indonesia, Iran, Iraq, Ireland, Italy, Japan, Lebanon, Liberia, Luxembourg, Netherlands, Nicaragua, Pakistan, Panama, Paraguay, Peru, Philippines, Poland (exiled government in London), Portugal, Spain, Switzerland, Syria, Uruguay, Venezuela.

In the following countries the Holy See has a representative at the episcopate of the country, called the Apostolic Delegate:

Australia (New Zealand, Oceania), Belgian Congo, British East and West Africa, Canada, French West Africa, Great Britain, Jerusalem (Cyprus, Jordan, Palestine), Malaya, Mexico, Turkey, Union of South Africa, United States of America. There is a special envoy in Ethiopia.

The following countries maintain diplomatic missions (embassies or legations) at the Holy See:

Argentina, Austria, Belgium, Bolivia, Brazil, Chile, China, Colombia, Costa Rica, Cuba, Dominican Republic, Ecuador, Egypt, El Salvador, Finland, France, Germany, Great Britain, Haiti, India, Indonesia, Iran, Ireland, Italy, Japan, Lebanon, Liberia, Lithuania (appointed by the pre-war non-communist government), Monaco, Netherlands, Nicaragua, Order of Malta, Pakistan, Panama, Paraguay, Peru, Philippines, Poland (appointed by the pre-war non-communist government), Portugal, San Marino, Spain, Syria, Uruguay, Venezuela.

CONTIGNATIO·TECTI·PARTIS·
VETER·BASIL·SVB·PAVLO·V·
DEMOLITAE·